MW01254622

A Tonalist

A Tonalist

Laura Moriarty

NIGHTBOAT BOOKS
Callicoon, NY

Acknowledgments:
A different version of the first two sections of *A Tonalist* appeared
in *Sal Mimeo #5*. The first section was also included in my *A Semblance:
Selected and New Poems, 1975-2007* from Omnidawn Publishing.
Another section appeared in *not enough night*, an online magazine of
Naropa University. Thanks to the editors.

Cover art by Norma Cole was done in 2003 as a gift to the author
Design by typeslowly

Library of Congress Cataloging-in-Publication Data:
Moriarty, Laura.
A tonalist / Laura Moriarty.
p. cm.
ISBN 978-0-9822645-6-0 (pbk. ; alk. paper)
1. Poetics. I. Title.
PS3563.O871635T66 2010
811'.54--dc22
2010006069

Distributed by University Press of New England
One Court Street
Lebanon, NH 03766
www.upne.com

Nightboat Books
Callicoon, New York
www.nightboat.org

Contents

A Tonalist · 3
A Tonalist Coda · 116
Sources · 140

for Norma

Provokes statement
As invocation aligning
Light with time as
Light fingered dawn
Made away with by
Lotus eaten
Head fucked with
Sound mind
Meridian and prime
Their empire
Our time
The home of time rose
Your hand in it
My love

A Tonalist

1. Spectrum's Rhetoric

Light changes the sentence. A subject persists in memory
sounding. Walks along the edge of the continent. Tea leaves
piled like seaweed in a cup in a mind pink on the inside and like
the sea dark. Cut orchids and peonies as writing or going out.
Green of stems. Green of the sea. A long drive. A longer walk.
Movement is aloud.

"It is just this moment of red mind . . ." [Dōgen, *Shobogenzo*]

You as an address various and specific know where you are. Who
you are. But what do I know? "What do I know and when did I
know it?" you ask later. More on that.

A hill looms like a wave of earth. El Cerrito goes down to the
sea, the bay, nearby. The hill intimated by the name is in Albany.
Here. In California. Goes to the sea. In green. The sea white.

The city in the distance
Surrounded by

Color drains from it as light recedes but the color remains in this
Western version. This version of the West. That being the point
(of light visible as) (it is) made complicated by the physicality of
thought.

"the circumstances
like a fabric ripping
inside the body"

[Norma Cole, *a little a & a*]

But what is the West? What is light? What is empire? What
color? The body as light as perceived from the inside out. The
arrangement of color. The arrangement of time. Local time.
Thought as action. For time and color's sake. As read. Among
the hills golden and yet not empirical or not merely so or
empirical and yet not empire, though of it. But what happened?

"I saw the
countryside

for seconds like
a film thru"

[George Albon, *Empire Life*]

What happens to make us believe what we see. To see what we
read as being read we write in color.

"Our best research is left with its mouth open."

Reading a diary backwards. Writing it. Writing the experience
before having it. Thinking of an indistinct town from a distance.
Of the city. Thinking about the war in a store in the midst of the
empire. Thinking about Cornell, not the boxes but the diary. The

lack of sentimentality in his Romantic Museum — or the mad
presence of sentiment. Or its ephemerality.

In Eisenstein's *Romance Sentimental* a woman plays a black piano
in black and then a white one in white. She sings an old song of
longing. Handwritten explosions come later after the branches
rush by and the sea is included. There are monsters.

"I may forever lose the light . . . " [Kamau Brathwaite, *Zea
Mexican Diary*] "If she should die . . . I may forever lose the light
the light — the open doors."

Aspens like sequins (for example)
Unlike lichen
An arrested splash
Green and light green
Or black with white
The lichen yellow and black

"I don't know where you buy it or whether there is a premium for
buying it. I don't understand how to do it or use it."

The Lotus Sutra

The body in its place
Hybrid of door and face
Present text to be
As you are there then where
Transcribed in its entire
Repetition each day

More patient than anyone
The act of
Who speaking moves
Gives her notes away

"The act of remembering or the vibrations of the sutra
Crash though the real world"

[Philip Whalen, "Four Other Places"]

We see to the bottom of the lake. The stems deep among white
rocks. Green and red leaves flat on the black water. Green to
yellow. Yellow lotus buds. Leaves furled. Magenta inside. Spread
out on the lake. Blue now of the sky. Black and green of trees.
Beauty of husband nearby. Lotus and trees in the background.
Husband. Half lake half sky.

Untitled

Mariposa lily

Black and white

Lotus ubiquitous there (East) as here the cross. (West.) It is
not about death, suffering or sacrifice, but about cultivation,
recitation, transcription, translation, genre, gender switching,
mud and light. The bright things that grow there.

Darkly

But silent

Stance

Among the Buddhas in my mother's album is the wooden one
in Berkeley Zen Center pictured with a vase of columbines,
a candle and a small statue of Kwannon. The altar for our
wedding. And here we are kissing.

Years missing

Intervene when

Startled from sleep by the wind, I see again the peripheral
beings I have lately noticed but who I can't see if I look directly
at them. Rows of monks. Known to be Western monks. Rows
of pale green robes. Green monks. Eastern but Western. Yellow
lotus.

Merely a phenomenon of sight.

The house alight. Water on the floor. The house is empty or
needs to be emptied. The room is filled with glasses, keys,
keyboards, pillows and cups. It is dark. There are too many
bright things. There was a party. A wake. Cabinets are open and
broken. What can we do with this place? What are we doing
here?

Hereinafter

Things given

Come back

The glass elephant in the painting of the lilacs floating in the
photo like a thought over the three of us, my aunt, my mother
and I on a couch. My mother's eyes, as if to say "Okay. What the
hell. Here I am alive."

"I hold you like a river."
[Esther Tellerman, "Mental Ground," translated by Keith
Waldrop]

Like heaven falling, the long line of cloud heads directly for us.
It spills over our hill in slow motion. We see the fog in shreds
above and descending. Next day we watch as it lightens and
dissolving, we pull away.

Wandering at the bottom of the ocean of air, reading two
slim volumes. One a translated revelation, the other about the
weather.

"And I saw a new sky and a new earth."
[Revelations 21:1;][Revelations 20:11]

"And books were opened"
Bleeding meaning
Body in time
Just as we said (read)
Red thinking but not

[8]

Speaking though speaking
Enough to say

Bleeding meaning in a hospital on Earth sitting — a skinny
Buddha with good hair. I meet your famous friends and say
Tonalism with you and you say "Good." "Title." We agree right
there referring to past and future with sweeping gestures. You
point to light with the hand you have making

"The highest heaven in the world of forms form"

The painter in the painting. The gray clouds of paint behind the
mailboxes like her smoke. The black trees. Her signature in the
corner. Legible. I did this.

The name affixed I see

Drains the life

Roars into me from another world

But that painting is unsigned. The autograph is in my mind.
This is not my mother. These are not our mailboxes. They are in
the country, in fact, in the clouds. Ours were on the base, by the
house, on a street. I can't remember them. I can't read this.

People with colors

Arrive and grieve They leave

The receptacles Have left

Petals scattered

Old sunlight. Morning fire. She dreams that she speaks. The
lines of the sea. The distance is complete. The creek swollen.
Oaks with moss hung. The sweep of light from the lighthouse
as approaching on Highway 1. Lens, headlight, windowlight.
The trees braided impossibly upward. A gold rectangle on
transparent blue. Thickly pictured. The lens was invented by a
French physicist. This was his room. This, his bed we sleep in.
This *we*.

"The landscape
is the portrait of
the sun. Only
skin is skin deep."

[Norma Cole, *Spinoza in Her Youth*]

I can hear as well as see the quiet as you sound it in your mind.
Is it my imagination? Is it your speech? A change occurs during
the sound. The colors are audible. The sea disappears into the
afternoon through a line of gray leafed blue gum. The green
is green. The light dark. The artificial log burns down. Books,
notebooks, and I reflect like television in the glass doors of the
fire. Reading (watching) Alan Halsey's *Memory Screen*. Fire
sucked by wind. We take the measure of it. Screen and wind
and I. Read him. Read you.

Lyric intimate of
Eucalyptus

The green countryside
Comes out of my head

 Writes as taken
"I was taken"

The green (me)
Surrounds (you)

Each of the characters rests on a lotus. There are slight variations
in the flowers. The late sun makes the rocks seem young. For
now we will remember everything in advance. I never knew this
was the beach of that dream. The cove of that love.

Are we different from the sun? Seeing the rocks through the sea
like a window to the present. "Renunciation of fame, fortune,
power and security." Why not? Why do we want what we want?
What do we do? We are not lyric but transitional. Not sun but
sung. Not color but of color. A flock of crows standing sounds.
Or gulls. A row of rows. "Bowing to the Buddha while being
annoyed by demons."

Basalt foam and
Rocks clapping
Damp sand and saw grass
Occluded trail
Jet like transparent meteor

Wave by wave
Roar of highway

Strong tea to hand
Tangled ganglia
Tops of trees
Things thoughtful here
Sun suddenly
Next day same fire same trees
Reading Niedecker
Spreads herself out on a field

"A good map will represent most of a lifetime's fieldwork."
[Oliver Morton, *Mapping Mars*]

What is Tonalism or as often — so-called Tonalism? Did it exist even when it existed? Can an idea of it be used to think about a contemporary phenomenon in writing? A Tonalist thinking. Originally, there was an emphasis on color, on a monochromatic approach and landscape. The person is the color of the landscape and is lit. There is a sense, a sensing, of light during transitional times of the day, transition itself, a muted but glowing experience of color. Craft as in the act of bending waves through time. The activity is precise.

The image is saturated with absence if, as most often, there is no figure. Or if a figure is present, it is alone. Or if there are figures, as with Xavier Martinez's *Apache Dance*, which depicts a bar in Paris, women and men are incandescent together, their backs to us, something between them besides light. Not landscape but just escape. The movement of the mind through color and time. Working through the didactic into the seductive. Decorative, as in pattern for its own sake — repetitious, emblematic, literal, local, but generalist in its sense of locale. Not the snap shot but the establishing shot. California. Drama of air, light, water and color. An emphasis on light, for which read sound. Color is sounded.

"No, it is not a collage. Hell flowers." [Spicer] "What you call collage I call thinking" [Halsey]

Gottardo Piazzoni's Tonalist obsession with the moon. Going to the top of an East Bay hill to view it with his family, cheering as it rises.

"[A]lways with the sense of mystery and savagery that appear to mark the artist's work." Thus Lucy B. Jerome orientalizes Xavier Martinez in the San Francisco *Call*. Martinez was a prodigy. He asserted his Mexican and Indian heritage in his painting and his writing. Did he think of himself as Lucy thought of him? Or as Tonalist — or as A Tonalist — in being not the nonspecific person but one saturated with color — with subjectivity, identity, physicality, sex, race, health, age. Rage.

James McNeill Whistler, the erstwhile grandfather of Tonalism, once wandered by Martinez painting in a Paris museum and said something like, "Good job." But the A Tonalist posited here is irreconcilable with Whistler's arrangements, his whitist "art for art's sake." His arrangements in white, women in white, symphonies in white. His infamous mother (arrangement in gray and black), his Irish lover (purple and rose) later discarded for his wife. This patriarch of that old Tonalism commented that "the future of art is in the hands of women," but he was so obviously, as they say, a hound. He was musical (with his terms) and ambitious. Vicious with both men and women. Ripper connection. More on that. "You also, our first great" [Ezra Pound, "To Whistler, American"] "Show us there's a chance of at least winning through." Or not winning. Not that. But this. These.

"Magnificent pink roses, chrysanthemums in a Greek vase, the color spectrum's rhetoric in an untranslated book, apocalyptic wallpaper for the classroom. Patience. There is a comet tail, a yellowish drip of unconscious brush stroke to the right. Have a drink. Blackness is before you and black is your favorite color. Honk. A customer will haul the installation away. Even now this gravedigger cruises on an ocean liner. He teeters on the edge of your work. Objects unrecognize you. The East is empty, there is nothing left to the West except the past, which is groundless night, a mass solution (like panic) to solitude, an imperishable escape. Let's go to Paris. Let's live, therefore we'll think. We'll be admitted to the best seats at the Opera, indicted for treason, encouraged to seduce our new enemies, become diplomats, say grace with trackless courtesans. There are dull beatitudes and reanimated brains. Houdini. The art of dissemination is the sign of the prodigy."

[Jerry Estrin, "Citizen's Dash," *Rome, A Mobile Home*]

The inward present. The indefinite maintained as a kind of discipline. Abstract simplification. Not arcane and yet there is a suggestive darkness. A realism of forms which melt into each other. Spiritual realism in which spiritual is defined as a formal practice relating to a belief in love but not of a person. Or of a person. And realism is verisimilitude in drag.

A finely dissonant harmony asserts a relentless quietism. Luminist white rock, another white and black as if written, still another darker white with green lines and areas of lighter green like land masses. Black like the sea.

Not a movement so much as a mood, an orientation, a realization that much that seemed forbidden is in fact required. Doubt, for example, especially self-doubt. A man can be in love with his equivocation. He can be equivocal about his doubt. He can use his knowledge against himself.

"Choked with interval of ecstatic doubt"
[Andrew Joron, "Anima, Macula," *The Removes*]

It is the beginning of the century. There is war all around. There is an empire. New media dominate the age, changing the old, replicating patterns of thought outward until they are discernable only to those morbidly sensitive to pattern. Information migrates. People are left behind in the wars.

Pont Neuf from below. Xavier Martinez. His life in Paris. Yellow light. Dark silhouette of a man, mist and smoke. The sky is the color of the meditation wall. Five points of light, one of reflection.

Hazing over during the drive
Actual bridge remembered trees
Remembered islands and streets

Glow on the western horizon. Clarity of sky drained of color
after steady movement through the point out into the bay and
back. White against darker white.

Wingspan pictured
While the wall resting
Into itself and the purple
Remains of the storm and spring
Feeds the pond deepens
Swarms with tadpoles
We in the mud go beyond
And up into the cliff
And forest meadow
Great Blue Heron

Black and white reduces everything to tone. There is no color
but color. There is light and dark. Heron bent as stands, folding
up. Time and light again. "Thanks to our ability to stop we are
able to observe."

[Thich Nhat Hahn, *Breathe! You Are Alive!*]

Not stopping but going out into
Inner reaches of San Pablo Bay
Point Pinole was Giant Station
Another East Bay dynamite factory

Always blowing up
Oceanic perspective
Pebbles to rock and back again
Eucalyptus, bay laurel, evergreen and oak
Large remnants of the world on the beach
As if after the war as if
The war were ever over

Only the objections
Rusting toxic ghost fleet
On its way despite
Were ever over
Our belief in that ocean

Faint with color
I have seen you
Faced with color
Glazed successively through which light
Penetrates and is reflected back
As a formal relationship or
Paradise cult boundary
The letter (your letter)
Between heaven and earth
Anything could have happened
But the particle stays fixed
Space and time fluctuate around it
(You don't die)
To be a fact is to
Reason from the bottom up
The old problem of telling time at night

"Forget subject matter," they say
"Forgotten," we reply but it's a trick

And again dreaming a phrase

Time and light
Having gone on
Because alive
Drenched with

Dawn after green-lit dawn
Or goes down
Whose bombs fall
Into the muddy world
Whose time goes on

Alexander Helwig Wyant, Tonalist, had a stroke at 42 while
traveling out West. His right hand was paralyzed. He taught
himself to paint with his left hand. It is a somewhat looser
technique. He was known for the fluid brush and restrained
palette he came to from the Barbizon school. He died in '92.

Sixteen breathing exercises
Four establishments of mind
Body, feelings, mind and objects of mind
"looking deeply to shed light"

"336 symmetries, the highest possible number for a surface of
genus three . . . The Eightfold Way in marble is divided into
seven-sided patches" that one can feel to exist, as rubbing they
continuously change into each other and also

[18]

Fringed blossoms of eucalyptus
Tulip trees, oak and acacias

Objects and events at the origin

Well inside the body
Memory with desire

Not the sea
The sight of the sight of the sea

The body seeing sight
Seeing scent

"Scent

        the simple

                the perfect

order

        of that flower

                water lily"

[Lorine Niedecker, "North Central"]

One claims light
The other dark yet

Seem to be the same
Statement because arranged

As parallel universe do exist
For example yours and mine

Like beams that won't meet
Until space curves or times ends

There is never any time
Even now it seems gone

As we fall bodily from line
To line it is quiet

The sound of my head in your voice
Each word alone with the other

Sounded out as in
I should have told you

Once more from the top
Nothing is what I wanted

2. [   ]

Breaks apart
The world as vessel
Everyone dies
A craft flies on which we are
Massively dependent
Like the world
Fragile and expensive
Shot through with

Lotus root
Lotus eaters whose
Appetite inundated with
The memory of
The feast before the feast
Of talking of taking
From it a new thing
The air with light
Shakes the leaves as wet through
The camellias in their bright
Morning (said) (Raworth) last night
"Tomorrow I die"
Startling those few among
The company remaining wonder
If true

A Tonalist, international but local, like yourself. Related, relating to color or light in all its manifestations, including tone. Relating to tone as sound. Sounding out. An acknowledgment that song exists. Song exists as color. That songs exist in history not to compete with other songs but to make audible the (a) symmetricality of thought, meaning sensation. Each category splays and empties like a river into the heart. Absorbed or sinking into. Blood. Color.

Your pleasure in finding information in the form of sound. Your value for listening, believing perhaps that it is less mediated than reading. That something read is not as immediate as something heard. One must be still in reading. It fixes the eyes, requires a narrow choice of postures. By a trick of consciousness reading seems less physical than hearing or seeing, though it is arguably more athletic. Though reading is not a sense, is it not sensual?

Pessoa's Sensationism of himself making
A movement of one with one and one

For Pessoa read person who is not Pessoa

Read forest floor for airport bar. Bay laurel root system. Airport trees. Scattered skies. Dispersal and arrangement. Reading matter. *Always Astonished.* Loss of self in text. "To feel is to create." Did he believe that? "Holding opinions is not feeling." And " . . . given that the Universe has no ideas." "What is feeling" but the idea of feeling felt by an ideologue who contradicts his selves? Who asserts an esthetic of contradiction. An anthology of selves who come out like "In evolution, we do not find a regularly ascending line; on the contrary, development takes place in a violent and

cataclysmic manner, in which gains are achieved only through
fundamental losses." [Fernando Pessoa, "Letter to Marinetti"]

Serpentinite loud rushing
Diablo green air
Oak, laurel, pine, manzanita
Leaves and needles steep
Oxygen sea silver or sun
Briefly the line
The top of another mountain

Mere nature brings about a hum in our thinking. Continuously
we walk in tune shedding the experience of others' regard or
disregard. Judgment already passed over like sky. We read them.
They read us. But they are not here now and later also will not
be. Already forgotten. The sky makes the day into dusk.

A wall of dark falls
Predawn prehistory
The occasional body
Sings us awake

Waking to sensation
Blue concentric flame
Dark because prehistory
The occasional body
Sings us awake

History starts up again. A morbid awareness of language keeps
it from seeming real. The nomenclature laced throughout a torso
at times erect or supine. Disarrangement reads as pain. The

scenario precedes the scene or job as it is called. What it takes to stay awake.

"Everything we need to know is right out in the open."
[Renee Gladman, *The Activist*]

The book, active in this case, is a relief. A belief envelops an attention as human love or active as in original. From a source assumed to be, to have been and remain warm or active and awake as music also — story in this instance — melodically corroborates our experience and intuition of events which then, like us, survive to occur in the next moment and go on.

"The Odyssey is the least boring of the minivans."

To read therefore to move is our action
I was moved (acted) by hearing your questions
Lines of the face legible as
Pain but in the good sense
Creased as crinkled
Concentrated like paper
Tearing along

"But the car is actually driving us."

Will the words of the question, if fully stated, if sufficiently elaborated, if sounded, if pressed. Will these words constitute an answer? When did you first begin to write? Why did you continue? When did you stop?

In mid-sentence the light
Dangerous for any vehicle
In mid-air where now our situation

Requires us to ask what expression means or whether we value
it as we have assumed we do not except possibly as a way to get
somewhere or to get rid of something. I wanted to demonstrate
my willingness to divest or to be divested of but couldn't stop
just then. Listen.

Again the wall but not yet
Day is expected
The blinds and eyes open to
Each other
The effect of light on thought
Time to go

The voices in the song separate becoming distinct like opinions.
It is the dead of day. What did you expect? One can't argue with
nature. The interaction of sound with sound. The orchestrated
version. Water with water.

In the old days
It was the complexity of an iconographic relationship
That allowed it to take place in plain view
In the new days the new relationship
Everything is always plain
Like mud we "with sound say
in phone light back to a totally wet detail"
[Jerry Estrin, *In Motion Speaking*]

[25]

Dead and then dead

And only in that event
As in a mudra taken consciously
As when hands hold
A form of thought filled with doubt
An expedient gesture in which
There is no limit
In scenes from different perspectives
To the number of points you can earn
The figure at the left

The unidentified Buddha
Of a lost text
The lower part of the body
Parasols and fans
A pedestal under a canopy
A lotus or tomb or paradise cult
Though possessing a wife
Though eating and drinking
Though easily beguiled he retains
Prestige among philosophers
And will lead us somewhere
Episodically

The average man who commissions these icons has in his mind
the sense of the flowering and understands it to be circular
and temporary. The exceptional man is circular and temporary
himself.

"Just drive."

3. (Dis)solution

Let's talk about the sky
The triumph of night
In the form of a mask
A muralist of the bruised
Body trembles along the strings of
Dissolution framed as
Appearance reappears
I am you he claims
Behind rows of fruit
The street beats like my heart
But you don't believe me
You simply don't
Though the spectrum
Indigo is for example
An experience of color like ink
Writing absorbed by writing
Colorlessly

Let's talk about the sky
These two elements together but
Which two finally air?
Water and sound or light?
Transit horizon edged and overlaid
With storm sun or head

Lights of a dead thing dizzy
Background falls away
Born down with continuing
Continues also with cars
Horizons move in and out
Another progression occurs
On the side that you are on

A body beats like a street
As one who does not
Find himself on a side
Trampled because driven
Stiff because dead
Coming at you like night
Cut edge of spring
Grasses or flowering now or later
The white screen remains
Sounded but visible
Let's talk about
He explains
His presence with the sky

A piece of it torn out with mountains attached and pasted into
a letter. We regard changing light together in the afternoon.
We identify the changes as what we mean when we speak of
one whose work is filled with light. We wonder together if A
Tonalist, taking care not to define it or ourselves in or out of
existence, though we know we exist. "It isn't pretty," you say,
motioning toward your cane when we speak of who we are
right now in words and gestures and an intuitive exchange of

shared history. Words accumulate later on a page, many of them not having been spoken at the time of their speaking. You point to your head and say of the words they aren't there but I can see you thinking.

We say the word conversation with pleasure and expectation. We speak of various men. You say "They are doing what they have to do." You include the concept of "No fate" except in the next step taken.

The air finds its way into the sun
Onto *Paris Walker*'s pink dust jacket
Stanzas for Iris Lezak pinkly also
Blake baking in it
And moves around the room in time
Visible on folders of paper
The pens and lenses
Rome, A Mobile Home
Assembled while dying
A portable universe
In retrospect alive with death

Sol justitiae
The crushing strength of a body
On a rock intoning in beefy darkness
Its impervious gesture

[Estrin, *Rome* again]

[29]

The clouds molest me
In the baroque dark
Furniture lit from inside
Illuminated by form and by
Recognition of form as
We live by each other

You can't argue with the sky
Not apocalypse but morning fog
Low upon and obscuring the usual
Sun as we wait for it to come up
For the war to begin
And the world to end

When the light falls on the floor
Goya's light on Goya's dog
Sinks into frames of memory
Suggested but not seen and then seen

We go back to the clouds
Something printed in Spanish
Cursive or again red
Penmanship or the torn edge
Of a letter (*carta histórica*)
A portrait of one reading
A series of maps and animals
Something unbelievably green
Obelisk or cenotaph
A final noun surrounded

A Tonalist like yourself might object to a strategy transparently
failing to be opaque when density is so much what we have
sought in our speaking. The hidden views are the ones we should
expose. Untitled columns shimmer in my head. I lived in that
thoughtful palace among pillars white as Piazzoni's moon

The clouds again threaten I think in Spanish. Their longing for
repetition and confidence is the one being satisfied now. The
betrayal will be later. Clouds and mildness are the context for
this conversation. This cold doesn't confuse me. It's spring.

I come over and we talk about the sky.

4. For now

Hand held vehicle

We are in a casualty-producing environment. More on that. All the floor covered with color. Is this freedom? I don't know. What if you are a poet? What do you do?

There is a sampling of rain. There is a storm but no rain. There is no moisture (but the blood on the floor). I can't speak the names you say. I dream you are my doctor and I can't say the names of the places we are in or the people we know. You fly a short distance in a plane in the dream. You use an open book to suggest landscape. There is a picture of a maze. When our appointment is over, you turn away. You say

"I am dazzled by a Frankish woman"

"All violence is injustice," I say [Thich Nhat Hahn]

"Her eyes are as blue as the steel of a lance"

The war is over in advance. The demonstration goes on. You go on. Riding through enameled tunnels of light, we arrive at an impasse. We make a lot of noise. Someone alone in the tunnel approaches. Everything requested has happened.

His skull was missing when his tomb was opened. There are
no written sources. For what we know. We dream a city. This
holy city is sensitive, crucial, irritable, and easily startled. It has
difficulty concentrating and is pessimistic. It is being bombed
night and day. It stays awake while we sleep. It takes more air to
sleep than the city has. The city has

Sunk into the horizon
We get time in trade
For what we know
You have to do something
We drive away

The approach at night vast trees illuminated by headlights.
Branches reticulated like maps remain vivid in the morning.
Staring as if seeing into the city in the distance where still asleep
the city dreams of me.

You have to do something. You claim not to write poems
anymore if you ever did. It's all pictures, you say, meaning
the effect of light on light. Or inscriptions. The effect of lines
on line. You note, frame and detach (I add) the sections from
themselves. Ignoring the divisions except the arbitrary ones. I
understand what you mean by the word hand though you haven't
said the word but the gesture is evident. The light is stunning on
the narrow bay before us. But will it stop the war?

"Be polite. Be professional. Have a plan to kill everyone you
meet." The president at his country retreat rests. We rest. A gull
settles. Another egret. Another regret. Another war.

They dig up the bodies with their bare hands

How can they fly that slowly?

"like shadow act"

[George Albon, *Empire Life*]

"The opening
of the chro-

matic world,
step taking
each un-
foreknown, the

turn, color,
direction, sign."

[Albon, *Empire Life*]

There is a need for as much air as possible among the lines.
Behind them. Words are specific and ordinary. Not everyone
but someone in particular. If A Tonalist were music how would
she sound? Atonal? Would she be a song? Next door lovers
speak quietly. There is reticence. There is insistence.

Hand to hand

Retaken

Vultures the pier

The sphinx of *Mars* on the cover of your book has your face and
eyes. I recognize the wave and the shape of your shoulder. The
curve of your tail. Feathers like hands splayed.

The trails merge

Thiasos Apollon Dionysos

A man leaves a sign of himself

Memory order passion

Heavy fighting in suburbs

Vanquished on the narrow trail by pink bells. Blue star vines
curl. Snakey mud of estero below. Blackberries fruitless because
spring but budded. Climbing around the mud. Sliding into it.
Extremely slippery conditions.

"The woman is speaking."

[Norma Cole, *Mars*]

With bewildering speed

Realists can see

refrain

"colors around her

colors surround her"

[Again, *Mars*]

With bewildering speed

Realists can see

Fierce, stubborn or surprising resistance

When resistance occurs

It occurs for thee

"for Laura

'all the colors silently'

with much love,

Norma"

5. The Visitation

Early sun and then gone
Birds on the job already

In *Spinoza In Her Youth*, Norma comments, "lyric is a continuous
beginning / again" and "Can a fiction / write a fiction?" mingling
those questions and genres. Can one not?

Intimate address. Acknowledgment of what shared humanly as
restlessness with the present, disbelief in (but commitment to)
identity, one's own or that of one's adversary. A government is
adversarial is intimate, entering the house by means of bombs or
soldiers, taking things away. As oneself. Taking from each other.
The sense of light entering the family window. The physical
presence of light makes us. See ourselves in a certain way. Or the
landscape is us.

We become darker as it gets later

"Against religious darks, a sense of utmost dark insiders"
[Taylor Brady, *Microclimates*]

Begs the question (exacerbating the sentence) (the silence)
Of who we are in relation to

"Cloudy Day" "Golden Glow" "California"

Tonalist darkness (1890-1930)
An idea settles over a color
Figures in a landscape range from gold to brown
A single color dominates the forms
Perceived through a veil of light

Time and light again
The "Visitation"
Of people with light
Charles Rollo Peterson
Call it California Gothic
Precursor to Noir
The effect of sight on light

"It is important to understand what we're participating in, to realize that we rest in darkness and experience vision. Many people take vision as a given and don't realize that they are actually seeing." [Nathaniel Dorsky, "The Illuminated Room," *Devotional Cinema*.]

In April during the war
We see what we believe
In April many are dying
Here in the sense of here in the world
But gone now
Mediated to death
Framed by furniture
The living becomes the dying room
Pictures just electrons until we see them

"I am no longer able to hold a continuous video in my Imagination"
[Yedda Morrison, "Untitled"]

May, June and July
Midsummer lack of night
Too much light too much

"Light an indescribable index

Figures of smoke trouble the infinite
Border that burns away"

[Jerry Estrin, *Rome, A Mobile Home*]

A deep nocturnal boulevard
Bright like water or a downfall

Anticipates August through a green tunnel
Cloud, mockingbird, owl

"[A]n infinite regress tunneling into the suddenly foregrounded
gaps in our municipal substance until the streets themselves grew
porous and the waters came up"

[Taylor Brady, again]

As much as can be carried we bring
In small bags away

6. A Reader

Whose robe falls
Opens the garment or form
Frames a torso that twists
As she reaches (reads)
Or pictured sitting sits
Also pictured the book

Also falling the robe opens onto a vista. The pattern of which.
Taken from elsewhere in a familiar act of piracy or editing,
isolated by commerce, is readable as part of a tradition going
back far enough for Europe and Asia to be irrelevant as
categories. Ghandaran Buddhas peer in stone with their Western
eyes, their Silk Road robes of rose granite. Or as here a creature
of the Pacific Rim wears what is to hand. Holds open the book,
clasping the kimono. To her.

For whom languor
Or language broken
The lines pitched
Spill over until

Composure rights itself
And cedes to thinking
A version taken from
Fan, fountain pen, letter opener;

Or open letter
Predawn and modern before the modern

Portrait of a wife by her husband and mentor *Lucia Reading* and
later Lucia Mathews' *Red and White* of herself looking into what
would be the camera if it were a photo but instead at us — an
arrangement of tones. For hours to be. Surrounded by a dark light
unconnected to anything but darkness whose page remains ajar.

She reads to see with what
Formal setting unseated
The right to bend

Lucia meaning light
This portrayal of a reading subject
Not of me by myself she claims
But of the you in me

A wind storm just outside
Her mind bent
Moon to planet or planet to
House swept by the wind
As if gravity were inside

Where she relaxed and alert
Changes (is changed) into

A hideous series of faces speak out of dancing
Bones whose form is familiar but unpredictable

"'The clothes make the man'" as the motto of the matter at hand
is what is different about the present reader (writer) who reads
(writes) when applied to the vast archives of possibility.

"Leonardo invents the paper airplane"
[Taylor Brady, *Microclimates*]

How was this done?
The problems are begging to be solved
From the origami point of view

The crumple zone as an issue
To unfold the wings as an act
Back out into space there are questions about
What the mind can do with a piece of paper
In situ always only present when

A version (the visions) come up again and again
A tradition more than a problem
We remember we are in childhood
With its hideous and prickly

"velveteen, wool, mahogany, yellowed paper . . . " [Brady]
The material means

"There is a lack of simplicity in the drama," she reflects. "And yet
it devolves, osmoses, morphs, yields, urges. It is not assaultive in
the fact of being too much though muchness is the least one can
say of it."

She is sleepy now. The text threatens to dream her if she would
only transpire visibly.

She is hot cold hot again
The subtropics unfold in breathless chunks of

"'your ill health insured strain
toward the next wide-open pen'"

He writes tellingly or scrawls
The "open" "pen" continuum being only one
Of the many dilemmas posed by the manuscript which
Reinscribed resists printing as if it were itself a process

Being written only where writing ends
Or composition

"of hackneyed pirate adventures" into a hot and storied
Climate of baroque amuse until

There is barely any day left and
Changing again the reader dressed and redressed
Contemplates the "dear reader" she has come to

Treasure unexpectedly
That by lamp-lit eyes

"Nonetheless that light, however ironically approached,
however dimmed and deflated by self-lacerating humor, was
the medium my sight clawed through as I taught myself to

[43]

read in the dead and stony dark, against which experience, or
rather the fact of having had an experience which was now
irrecoverably closed, like the smell of bougainvillea on the other
side of the cinderblock, had failed as yet to appear."

Where the explanation is worse than the disease we feel we
remember when we. We feel when we come to you with this
that you had better be. (Here Lucia pulls on long wool stockings
distinctive for their softness, their warmth and the tightness of
their fit.) Attentive.

"cover every surface . . .
of the noise . . .
as ends in themselves"

[Brady]

He attends. He transacts. But like Harlow in *Red Dust* his is a
compromised figure. "Don't run around here like that," he tells
her (Clark Gable) but she says she will stay comfortable meaning
bad in her case. Later, after the shooting, she reads to him.

We see this on our inner TV
As in Alan Halsey's *Memory Screen*

But I digress she admits
Of cross reading or
Laying oneself open to
Danger where it comes before
"bloom, the tomb" and points

[44]

Backward counter-intuitively
Setting the stage for the overlay
Of names, forms and fish previously
"Simple words, the waiting and call"
The broken glass picture suggests also
Again the idea of order or at least
Sequence which when it dithers into quince
Or queen acclimates into an ecology
As green as the world but more portable

So not remembered but carried around with
And needs to be seen to be seen
It is the function of the screen to divide and keep
As well as to read or might be in fact is
A screen saver with what
Piquancy such a scene can be associated
Or can in any sense be saved

A late hurricane makes its way
Into the sea between us
Rain followed by heavy rain followed
By a diagramatic display on another screen
Odette makes landfall and the book slides
From the silken lap of

Late morning repetition but not yet
As going forward in a sounded
Mechanics not felt so much as spelled
A stylus crackles in its groove

Absence is seen to have been contained
Where grave is not error but errant
Drawing us to within the hair's breadth
We breathe when we see
The Spicerian rabbit again pale

This garden's inhabitants are the citizens of a realm not exactly
permanent but less temporary than the pulsing beating world we
normally conceive of as being when breathing in smoky light we
listen to the alarms of the day from the disasters of night. We
can't stop listening.

Lucia is sleepy but awake in a half-lit position, she is caught
between things. She considers the antioxidant properties of
chocolate as opposed to tea (you as opposed to me). The song
she sings comes from your ears to my heart. The chimes in this
repetition are simplicity (repeating) itself.

She (he) abandons a lover, draws her back down and re-
abandoned she emerges as the subject of a series of tableaux
featuring her hair. Now twisted, now falling. Now shorn. Once
dark now gold and gray. An interior scene where the window
opens onto a prospect. The text reflects all this but the original is
less realistic. Only the words go on.

There is no backstory but the scene can be seen variously.
Whistler was accused of being slapdash, of "flinging a pot of
paint into the face of the public," but the face was not the part
of the anatomy that was the object of his fling. His was a stance
created or at least recorded in his observations of women, their

accoutrements and leanings. Until it became clear that he, like them, had to go, to be gone. In this case to Venice but it could have been anywhere water was present or any other source of the naturally occurring phenomena of the endless pattern for which we are all known. Lucia dreams of Whistler. She whistles him.

And then again waking she realizes the garden she is in the one she must eat if she is herself to go on. She sees the problem. She goes on ignoring this advice but as will happen she (waking) becomes what she reads. "You are what," she thinks, beginning to reason backward from the constitution, the consummation of eating. "You are what." You read:

"the tinseled hostless

surrounds him   endless anonymous capacity for entrance

"

And so enters
Crop by Yedda Morrison
Through the letter of
A measure of what rules
(The mouth of its own song)
Who eats what around here
Causing them (her) to exclaim

Oh no and again finds
A new line meaning the wrong thing
Has gone down

The garden is the horizon in this
Action comes to terms with
Being in need of

Of the body by itself
When what really happens
Is known

But is knowing enough?

The fiction in the event
(We are) controlled by

What is not in the story but is suggestive of a time perhaps
Neolithic when intelligence ruled not as a matriarchy but maybe
bi or gynarchy as coexistent interchange of prehistoric gardening
and gendering or engendering practices. Not written except in
stanzas of earth and in stacks of crops then finally, yes, written
in columns of what harvested and what stored in warehouses in
rows or in boxes as of the prose here. What can be saved for the
future from the voracious present? What spent? Constituting
then something like good government, an economy existing
for a while as an activity and idea simultaneously and a long
possibility of renewal but something happens then.

"a *governing* Radius of Gyration
a *circulation* of Radical Thought

collective starvation
spacing between successive Holes
our own *allowable* Mercy Radius'

[Morrison, *Crop*]

As similarly there is a further suggestion that plastic pumps
may suspend or display or as we expect or can be seen as urging
or surging through and with.

Cusp by Jocelyn Saidenberg

"extreme burlesque evanescent ripples
the sheepish impact two bodies have on each other"

Reorganization which when the one
Already twice taken becomes

The brink of the edge of the day
As open ended as in anything

The profound discomfort of having let up
Even for a moment swallowing hard

To assuage what alone will equal
To flee and change at once that leaving

Will bring back fresh to get
"no longer an isolated system of loans and debts"

"I want a body without organs"

[49]

It is sunset in the winter of
The stretch made when admiration

Realizes it is dreaming the wrong dream

As eating in place of the sutra
In rare form

It turns out the last time
Was many times ago

Expressing a context of familial connection as when cousins leave
for the front as opposed to what is held back when writing/riding
(being ridden) out of town in this instance means the current war.

"meaning's evisceration. self-cancellation. self-penetration.
Inceptive"

What finally happens to families?

Adjusting to the present reading she is not sure she was right for
the part.
Or not in the moment the ideal reader (writer) but she was

Or experiencing surcease from or apprehension as to what can be
Felt or folded into her belief that
To read is to believe again

Adding a dimension to the dimensionless
She holds her mind in her hands
Allowing to slide the book that

Gives with and onto
A conjured city pictured in the Lotus Sutra
Here called
Golgonooza where she has often

Named by William Blake and in his thought (as in the sutra)
Not a destination but rather a stop along

And here she is interrupted by the presence of a lover
Of painting which she as a painted figure
Her expression impossible to read

As slowed down as things appear
On the way somewhere to sound the same

"Sound is a way of playing with memory."
[DJ Spooky :: That Subliminal Kid]

As if a goblin grinned up
Appearing like an eight ball

The letters in the word
Fathom by Andrew Joron

She again reads pulling away

That measure made
What used to be called
Prophecy turns back

(Turns her back on)

[51]

Unspoken enemies whose
Cries of animals

What used to be called
Distance

"a self-refuting silence" or
Realizes the speaking of what

Centers itself in the face
With birds in it

Articulate inhabitants
Surround the day

Intimated by a horizon
Whose distance remains

A cosmological portrait of
Who this could be whose

Communality of language is suggestive of the presence implicit
in the outcomes which comprise the emergent catastrophes
encapsulated here. These are mathematic, historical, nonobjective
and vexed. The question has been posed of whether the use of the
language implicit in this problem is appropriate given the nature
of the emergency.

There is change. Not of subject so much as of object. A word
becomes another but sounds the same or is contained in itself.

Sounds that are the same as nature are proposed and do what nature does, which is to propose. These incessant propositions destabilize the mechanism causing the distances (see above) to become relative. The universe beats like a heart for a moment as the declensions become apparent in what can be identified as the Spicerian present. As the object of this action word, you are then (shown to be) there (here). Also.

The Spicerian present is nothing if not evident in this equation. The gift that keeps on giving is the clap of recognition which occurs to celebrate the betrayal of absence that must already have happened. During which its corollary of enduring is given. This brings us again (have we ever left?) to the given as what is always confronted in the moment of the reading of the present difficulty. Which is not to hesitate to call a spade a space but to acknowledge the existence of that implement in that suit, shape or designation. Assertion continues and is undermined to the point of almost total negation. (The metrics outpace the message.) Of the almost total negation of the only one left who can make the case. We arrive at the next line exhausted but suspicious. Alive but dead. Wanted.

Thinly scattered frost concentric

"Earth's black table tilts below time."

Horizons coincide

Tricked into the distance

Like a sled dog trying to mush out of winter, we are about
to be sacrificed to the prime directive of the presiding
omnipotence whose continental awareness far exceeds our own
mere mammalian illusions. Or it is simply dark. Permanight
immobilizes a trajectory whose tragedy was inevitable from the
first bark. We are the superior beings now. Able to shrink the sky
and traverse reason with the aid of our furry colleagues. We have
exceeded our dreams.

Or does it mean "howl with laughter?"

Someone says to Allen Ginsberg

In the century just

Past as the afternoon now old

Glitters like a hotel in the terror of the evening

Freshly defenestrated

"What happens here?" people say as falling

The literal sun now gone

But what do they want?

The universal option to be unfinished in the sense of unending,
dis(t)ended, disinterred, reentered, rendered, rented, defended,
resized, enfranchised, organized and undivided in a commitment

to free thought — not to be conflated with free trade or any other operations borrowing the word but unrelated or contrary to the concept.

"None of the / versions is complete or completable"
[Alan Halsey, *Memory Screen*]

Lettered to within or
Just off from
Alienate as in
The alien ate
Whole thingfuls of

The page as screen so that prosody exists in proportion to the proportions that the eyes see which is always true anyway. The eyes rest and see rectangles and golden sections and angular correspondences among words and letters laid out on the page. This is that page and yet isn't in the sense that there is an additional dimension — at least one. Or an element. Another time. The numbers produce the columnar appeal familiar to aficionados of the palaces remembered here. There has been some damage. But the pattern remains legible or eligible or at least the remains remind us. Not to go there.

"simple words. The waiting and calling"

Exist below what seems to be the source of the phraseology or is evocative of

Mouth where the mouth widens
Like a lens (or other sphincter) or wings
Which fits around space

Ivory of human
Keys come into it
The cream of "yellowed paper of" [Brady]

A round space
Unfounded or not subject to
The parable unfolded parabolic
To the list attached to the paragraph
Appended to the explanatory chart

A Latin green
Easy to see
Resuscitates the incident
Of the reassembled devils
Heads into the story of another book

As a face into an angel changes the angle of the take or turning
is a way to look at the next page. The days run away with your
heart fixed to the bones by the sea.

The destruction of writing having preceded the destruction of
reading or seeing betrays the transparency of the subject. It is
thus easy to see the green enter as everything empties out. The
survivor sorts through the detritus. The widow is the orphan of
the word window. The limits to the interpretive event produce
the line in the sand beyond which is the sea we all swim in. Here

at home is the mind of the land by that sea. The scale varies.
Gold is good. The fish turns to look back tangled as scales like
leaves open out widely. As if you could breathe through your
mind.

7. The Living Room

"Thought is a form of sculpture"

In answer to and as a reflection of
What is recognizable and yet not

Pictures of rooms in our collective
Biography accommodate the stuff (accumulates)

Of life considered as a form
Or the living room as an opportunity

Comprising the list of things in the room
The bibliography of this moment

Later or earlier or both
A bird heard from another room

Mocking my attempt to fall asleep
By mentally assembling the living room, piece

By piece, including the silver bowl
Damaged when my mother drove

Through the garage door and my
Tiny aunt rushed out saying "Goddamn,"

In a particular moment I picture both rooms
In my head we are on the couch posing

The photo of me with my mother and aunt, the one of Norma
with me and Bernadette Mayer, the endless snapshots of rows
of people on couches are part of what takes place in the living
room. The difference, one difference, between my aunt's couch
and the one in Norma's installation is that Norma's couch was
consciously chosen to fulfill its destiny as a couch. Norma,
Bernadette and I (or later Norma, Suzanne Stein and I (the
combinations are infinite)) fulfill our destinies by sitting on the
couch together. We know this while we sit, but we don't talk
about it.

"Which is blowing, the flag or the wind?"
Begins an action film by Wong Kar-Wai

Which is to say are we living
The room or is it living us?

Possessing us in an arrangement meant to evoke
The past but what if we weren't born then?

This is Saturday and that was Sunday
How far back can we go?

"It's the heart of man that's in tumult"
Wong Kar-Wai continues and in his film

The world moves and the actors are still
For a while until they too have to go on

"You feel like you've been here before" [A. Bird]
Norma begins on the floor

Starting her performance from a resting or prone position on the
somewhat grand staircase of the California Historical Society
(where the living room lives), Norma remains still while the
audience listens to a recording of her reading *Scout*. The work is
dense. She reads it rapidly. The quickness is in contrast to her
stillness. The contrast becomes more apparent when she rises
to a sitting position and begins to read. She has chosen words
that are currently difficult for her to pronounce. The stroke she
suffered in December of 2002 left her with a slowness of speech.
She was found on the floor. Whenever Norma stops reading,
Caroline Bergvall begins to read from a series of texts. Caroline
enunciates each of the letters in the words, performing them
slowly. There is a lot of assonance in Norma's reading. She uses
the word "violets." "Violence," I hear, thinking how physical
thinking is, how the body (how life itself) makes its own
violence, how sometimes things don't change as quickly as we
would like, how sometimes they change at the speed of (blood
or) light.

"The world-lotus blooms" (from *The Mudra* on
The bookshelf in the living room)

"In answer to and as a reflection of
The light of heaven" can be seen through

The glass in a view of the living room taken
From the street and the street itself

Is reproduced by the photographer,
Who is the father of Norma's son. The picture

Arrives in a flyer, I have it here.
"Are you are a writer?" she might ask

As you appear and you might be, you may have
Written there, as I do now in my mind though

In fact I am here where, though spring
It is cold and dark but green

Buds are everywhere of cherry
And hawthorn or poppies sharply

Wrapped like something unwritten
Or like a thing that's written but hidden

As when George Herms reads as part of
The exhibition he throws his handwritten and stamped

Poems into the audience (it's interactive)
Stamp, paper and poem all rolled into a ball

"exhibitions: temporary inhibitions, my semblables:
collective guilt" Norma reads from "Speech Production"

It's just another day in the world
The world is just another word like "Jack"

Which she also includes, adding "Why do I like it under the trees
in autumn when everything is half dead? Why would I like the
word moving like a cripple among the leaves and why would I like
to repeat words without meaning?"

She mentions her son Jesse in the reading and someone called JJ
"Bill," she says, and this is the end, "who was JJ anyway?"

It's spring now. Life goes on but the world ends
That we enter when we are in the living room

But it continues to construct itself backwards in my mind
The cloth texts from the "House of Hope" to detach and lay
themselves out

As I first saw them on Norma's floor before they were cut into strips
Like film and before I saw them and was filmed myself among them

Or actually taped making more tape to add to the tangled
Archives Tableau, the original of which we create ourselves

In a set of views that are personal and truncated
And might as easily run back- as forward

In the catalog of the show that followed his death, Montien
Boonma is quoted as saying that "The house is a metaphor of hope
that is impossible to grasp physically." In a sense, Norma's "House
of Hope" begins to be constructed when Nick and I go to the
Montien Boonma exhibit at the Asia House in New York in 2003.

We are startled by the beauty of it and the artist's insight into life and death. I like thinking about death with Boonma because he knew about it up close as I do, but even closer. One can occupy his sculpture helmets like rooms you can wear on your head. We give ourselves over to his thinking and to the fragrance of the sandalwood and herbs. He cultivated the image of the lotus and other aspects of Buddhist practice with an urgency that is relaxing. As with sitting practice, I find I can give myself unreservedly to the work and come away with the ability to feel more pain. The catalog we bring back for Norma is called *The Temple of the Mind*. Later the show comes to San Francisco. We go.

The living room is an atrium to the show
Giving onto a collection of works, worlds (words)

Impossible to grasp physically and yet impossible
To grasp any other way

"Thought is a form of sculpture." Joseph Beuys
As quoted by Montien Boonma

The show ends today
That began with this thinking

Laura Moriarty
April 16, 2005

But we are still
In the living room

[63]

Or in a series of them
As Larry Fagin's exquisite

And ancient cell with its
Modernist pink and red

Its antique black and green
Its abstraction and filigree

Is the flower sermon of which we speak the Lotus Sutra and, if
so, can we accrue from our speaking the merit from which such
reference is said to accrue? Or is it orientalism, but what if we
are Buddhists? What if we are enlightened by the sutra or for
some other reason or for no reason at all? What then?

Albert Pinkham Ryder watches
The moon over the Brooklyn Bridge

He is a character in a fiction
Angel of Darkness by Caleb Carr

People who know of crime write crime
Stories and those of us who know

Ambiguously write A Tonalist version
Or maybe it's the same thing

Inness and Blakelock, Ryder are
All associated with so-called Tonalism

But not labeled as such by their
Biographers, who note however the

"[H]eavy-lidded press of hazy damp
An obscuring but direct approach

followed by them. It allows for many thoughts to occur as one goes
from line to line, seeking but not limited to a series of conclusions
or to a cultivation of pleasures similar to those discovered in other
tonally ambiguous situations. It begins in the eye of the mind with
the movement among and between the points of reference. The
move is from the explained to the unexplainable, to the unseen
from the seen. "Art," Inness said "is not a thing of surfaces, but a
moving spirit." And yet, at the same time, at the end of the last
century but one, Maurice Denis famously commented that "a
picture, before being a battle horse or a nude, or some anecdote
— is essentially a flat surface covered with different colors
assembled in a certain order." Both dicta apply. The spirit of the
surface moves.

Inness attacks the medium itself
"Disfigured allusions to disfigured time"

His biographer says, quoting also the "seriality
And simultaneity of vision" noted by Inness

"Veiling, dimming, fading, occluding,
Obscuring, flattening, reconfiguring"

New views superimposed on other pictures
Thicken leading to an instability

And deterioration of the surface
And we are again ourselves dissolute

Left with nothing but the Dog Star
Sirius disappearing in preparation for a new

Season of walking and speaking
Among the weeds

8. The Imaginary Community

Real as thought
When thought

Plain as paint or
Audible sings

In tones that
In times which

These darknesses
Seem light

As among beings
Or notes between them

When us means both
Many letters

Between us
This commerce

As fast as light
Sets the tone

Webern's Bagatelles
The dark light again

As with yourself
Though (I am) not there with

But aware of (you) on
The edges of everything

To be read as if
Our lives depended upon

Knowing there is one
Are ones who know

"Bagatelle [French from Italian bagetella] — 1. Trifle 2. any of
various games involving the rolling of balls into scoring areas —
basket, hoop, net, goal-post, strike zone . . . Bingo! 3. A short
literary or musical piece in a light style." ["Philip Whalen," Bill
Berkson, *Continuous Flame*]

Musical, literary and artistic tonalities seem the same to me.
It's not just the synesthesia of the hangover from my most
recent migraine. I have always felt this way. Webern's Bagatelles
in which the strings organize themselves around the quiet
they produce and then insist on phrases that swell and fill the
attention before dropping again into a quieter mode seem like
Whalen (or Berkson) — light but precise, filled with the weight
of the difficultly lived life.

Bookend planets highlight
The early morning sky

Where birds wake and then
All day the birds

The French tulips red and yellow
On the table shooting stars are

Only in your mind the green
Of the explosion of twisted

Stems remind us of nothing
So much as ourselves

The community is inescapable. It is unnecessary to imagine
it. Even now it wakes, has its coffee, resists its cigarettes or
succumbs to them, deliciously, going to work. Today we look
forward to the party next week. We are so exhausted we can
barely speak. Except for me, who is taking the day off. Today
I am born. There were floods in Minnesota on the Mississippi
then just as there are floods in Ohio on the Ohio now, because
it's spring. Because it's spring and raining on the in- as well as on
the outside of my mind, I read and write in time to the dripping
and (much later) I'm typing and it's May but it's still spring and
things are still green because we are in love with the new and the
drying up and turning gold is late this year.

A group resists war with the arrangements
In their living rooms of things, colors

Colors are like words to him, they said of Inness
He is not one of them but it relates in that

Their concerns are domestic but lack the sentimentality
Rexroth later identified with the middle class which he despised

With a passion quite absent now that we are all more or
Less that and I am not talking about money of which I have little

But the suspension of the belief (mine) in the past in a class of
Artists or some beings like that who were outside the system

Where did we think we were? Or does someone still think
That way (maybe me)? The group in question is in love

With the new which in their case looks like the old
But curvier and brighter, more gay though they had little

To be gay about and though they had much,
Comparatively, in the way of money, or had more

Than ninety-eight percent of the world has, let's say,
And who in fact, "we," say, don't forget us, the other ninety-eight

Who work every day and watch shows where people
Like their jobs and solve problems because

There are few solutions but just one damned thing
After the other or there are nothing but solutions

As evidenced by the living rooms of the Bloomsbury
Group as beautiful as the idea of people as much in love

With freedom from war as they were with themselves
And colors were like words to them

And finally the rain is horizontal and petals are stuck to the glass.
We walk among the old growth ghosts and are reminded of our
dead. Saplings, lilacs and something else, oh yes, forget-me-nots,
are purple and black. It's a decade since the fire burned everything
here, though I remember it as clearly as if it was yesterday, and
now in a cabin on holiday I am layered in notebooks with tea
balanced on a pillow on a saucer of Hungarian porcelain. The
blue rim of the cup seems like the kind of detail about which
my community does not write, but I am sliding it in along with
Jacobus Boehme, who said, "What sort of triumph of the spirit
it was, I can neither write nor say; nor can it be compared with
anything other than with that which in life is born in the middle
of death, and it is comparable to the resurrection of the dead."
And it does happen to be Easter, though it's not god but people
who are coming back to me.

The living write notebook-like
Poems as this one or Taylor's *Yesterday's*

News which has a sense of event so continuous
And details of life so fully realized

That it attracts comment from Ron Silliman
Whose own continuity is notorious. Ron says

Eureka, Taylor Brady! And I am pleased, having said
Taylor to Ron a time or two

You use too many words I think (not knowing if of Taylor or
Ron) but I don't say it because I don't mind. Am I right in
imagining that you never mention the moon? Do you think the
moon is "over"? Anyway thank you for not bringing it up. For the
remainder of this project I promise not to mention the moon.

Word count
War criminal
Sap moon
Trance text
Hedge nettle
Spring forward
Fixed rate
Bishop pine
Plain song
Real words
Stand back

One can turn to the radio to get away from the dead but it's a
dangerous game. I hear that the CIA and NSA were both at
fault for allowing us to be drawn into the current war. Members
of their community speak on the radio. They speak in ways we
don't understand. No one wants to be a member of a despised
minority, even the government. People in the government have
feelings. They want to be collaborative, responsive and agile. For
them, falling back is not an option.

After the rain the wind
Storm after the storm
The tea the sea visible
Douglas fir, bay, oak in
Continuous motion like a poem

When I open Ron's *Under Albany* I come to the line "Jerry
Estrin never had a chance" and I object to it. He had the chance
he had. There can be a politics to cancer or to death but Jerry's
cancer was not politically inflected. Unless he got it because
living in Southern California in the fifties he was a downwinder.
Unless his mother got it for the same reason. But his cancer had
no symptoms until it did and then it was too late. I remember
being at a reading at Langton, sitting between Ron and Kit.
I told them both of Jerry's illness. By that time I was in some
sense used to the shock of it, used to not believing the words
I was saying but saying them anyway. They were stunned and
speechless. I don't know why I was surprised by the intensity
of their reaction. Jerry's chance of survival was .05%. I did the
research, but I never told him.

That day but "message deleted" I read
"I cannot forget you!" As a subject line

An obvious virus
So not really a threat

Not like forgetting which is too much
Or not enough and never not

A kind of twisting of the viscera
As those who know know

And further the books are edged with light like water as it falls
through the trees of Albany. "We of Albany," as Kathleen Miller
would say, if she lived here instead of Oakland. We of Albany
live among the birds and weeds and the sleepy concretions
of the bulb that stick out into the sea though it's just the bay
here. Gil Tract is in bloom with genetically altered plants, old
palms, Monterey pines and the ruins of an orchard. But as Mark
McGwire has said, "I am not here to talk about the past."

It's Memorial Day
Summer begins

The marble plaques of my parents' graves
In a vast military

Cemetery like the news of the day
Lists the dead from the war

Morning haze memory
Qualified by intervening media

Celebrating the war today
Remembering its cost

In *Silence* I read
"Atonality has happened"

John Cage writes "The term 'atonality' makes no sense. Schoenberg substitutes 'pantonality,' Lou Harrison (to my mind and experience the preferable term) 'proto-tonality.' And later "Atonality is simply the maintenance of an ambiguous tonal state of affairs. It is the denial of harmony as a structural means. The problem of the composer in a musical world in this state is to supply another structural means, just as in a bombed-out city the opportunity to build again exists." In Cage's case the solution is partly the meditative, notebook-like form he uses in *Silence* and *A Week of Mondays*. The books are iconic in the seventies when they appear. I first read *Silence* as an undergraduate at Cal. I regard it along with Blake's *Four Zoas* as a blueprint for my life. The ambiguity is the point. The use of the word tonal almost always includes this quality. Waves of meaning, color or sound are realized with a precision that belies the unsettling effect of ambiguity on reader, viewer or listener.

Serious series
Fraught thought
Satiated said
Observe obverse
Affective facture
Basking in baskets of
Bright dark light
Arresting rest

The community resists the war. Some are arrested. Activists are injured at the shipyards. In Iraq and Afghanistan, they are killed along with soldiers and civilians. You can volunteer to experience the war. You can resist. You can die trying. Try dying. Simple answers may not work. There's ambiguity. There is arrogance and greed. There are accusations and sides. When I say at a dinner to Semezdin Mehmedinovic that the situation in Bosnia was complicated, he looks at me as if I were mad. "It was not," he says.

"and the torrid sky appears
as the moon begins to shine amidst the war"

Sarajevo Blues
Translated by Ammiel Alcalay

Historical explosions occur
Around us all the time

We have been up for hours
Maybe days though it's early

We're traveling across time zones
Mixing tracks and occupations

This in the context of that
It's the least we can do

Larry Fagin is teaching a class on Ovid. He is thinking through Tiresias's seven years as a woman. The conversation we have at dinner at Shima near his house on East 12th begins with me saying that I am teaching for a change. Characters of various poets are discussed. I notice that one develops a generational take and retains it in relation to experience even as one becomes aware of (and is open to) new things. One is fully formed in relation to

certain givens, continuing, forever, to think and speak in those
terms. Then there are also the givens of people of like mind. A
sense of congruence is a pleasure, as when Larry says that he loves
cut flowers in vases and I say I also love them and that scientists
have just created a genetically altered blue rose.

The sun on the street from the west
Blinding silhouettes of the crowd appear

As the cutouts of heads Larry recommends
To transform Netflix into the movie theater experience

Crossing Manhattan again with many more
People than I think I see in a year here

I admit to Larry I don't have Latin, though I have claimed to have
the same edition of Ovid he is using, a red volume which I now
think is perhaps the Latin version. Why do I believe I have that
book? Where is it? Is it really red? Have I read it?

Forget everything about the book
Business I think to remind Brent

Going out for a croissant at dawn
The radio wakes me in Spanish

Newspapers tightly wrapped
On stoops it is warm already

We load our suitcases into the cab
And head for the show and finally

Continue our study of airports
And sports bars

Brent asks if I am from Sacramento. We are testing to see if we
remember each other's stories. I remind him that I am from St.
Paul and remember that he is from somewhere like Milwaukee
and grew up in North Carolina and Southern California. Brent
admits that though he often asks questions he seldom remembers
the stories he is told. Whereas I seldom ask but always remember
the stories though name of the teller will escape me. We talk about
form as we are boarding the plane. Brent asserts that change has
value for its own sake, by which he means variety of approach,
and further that the variousness of *Bird & Forest* could be even
greater than it is to better effect. I come out for consistency within
the book but change with each next project because I think of
that as what I do, though there is more change in some projects
(as this one) than others, or less, depending how you look at it. I
remind him that Jocelyn is writing a book of beginnings and he
remembers that he knows that and likes the idea. I say there is
something to be said for directionality

Too exhausted to speak
Or sleep we listen to

The strangely sourceless airborne
Radio or TV endlessly

I dream when I don't sleep less clearly.
"Too much emphasis on the tonal," the radio

Says, "creates a meandering quality
Complicating the experience of the auditor."

I count backwards from a thousand
Attempting to fall asleep or to fall

For or into something and though I don't
Sleep I do dream of the two snakes

In Ovid who change Tiresias to a woman and
Back again allowing him to compare

Men's to women's pleasure
He claims women's is better

Becoming as a result (changed by Juno) blind
To everything but the future

In the future, I prepare a talk about Blake's engraving of the
Greek statue of Laocoön, a Trojan priest and his two sons. He
surrounds the image with an aura of aphorisms that assert his
poetics. I find again, in the engraving, the two snakes. Here
they come up from the sea to kill Laocoön and his sons. I talk
about the physicality of being drawn down into death and about
practice. "Without Unceasing Practice nothing can be done /
Practice is Art If you leave off you are Lost." Blake engraves this
statement around the desperately outstretched arm of the dying
father. The snakes pull him down. I give the talk at Naropa,
looking out at the community. Some have, like myself, lost
people. Some of them find me. I find I am connected to the

"Nothing" of this practice and to the practice of the outside (as Blaser names Spicer's way) or Blake's relentlessness.

There is always transformation. Life and movement are not different. That the suffering of Laocoön and his sons is normal seems strange to me and remains difficult to remember. One is oneself the mnemonic device. Just as the system produces the virus that destroys it (cf Jacques Coursil), we comprise our own fate. I mean compromise. More on that. There are four Noble Truths, five conditions, an infinite number of other truths, stipulations, conditions, corollaries and conclusions. They can't be said in too many or too few words.

One suffers

To desire is

Three stopping

For the way

What doesn't exist can cease to be. It seems like a contradiction but that's the way it is. We try to fall back on something but just keep falling. "Nothing takes forever," we think, but think again maybe that is exactly what Nothing takes. Today we are going to the country, so we picture trees — not specific trees, but the eternal trees of George Inness or the eternal forms of Blake. They were not Buddhists but Swedenborgians believing in a reverse hierarchy of heaven, hell and eternity. We have in common with them the concept of the fallen world, called by Buddhists

Samsara. Here we find the individual trees.

On the trail we see
The riparian give way

To the meadow and then
Forest community

Day to night
To night again

Heat to hot
As the world burns

Us to them
You to me

9. Bulb Maze

"His own stylized pain, unmixed colors and simplified forms
in black were very influential."

The bulb is a maze

This partly concrete version includes
Dynamite along with historical
Explosions and the sense of jutting
As a jetty goes out into the sea or the
Granitic cloud pattern of a rusted iron
Anchor anchored in concrete rests Rust
Having been another name for this town

But a vision is not a policy

"A flower sermon:
critique is like a swoon" [Ron Silliman]

Is it the lotus?
Or any other flower that

Reminds us by death of the real. I am
He claims just another land(e)scapist or

Absentee lyricist fitting words into
The nooks and crannies of the melody [Andrew Byrd]

The book is WHAT the claim is made up
The interview is on the radio

"The landscape is a negotiated solution to multiple needs."
[*Delta Primer: A Field Guide to the California Delta*, June Wolff].

The song is a joke. Just east of the Bulb and at the end of this
block, Gil Tract is a vestige of the farmland that once abutted
the houses, dynamite factories and dumps of this mile-square
town, just north of Berkeley, well to the west and south of the
Sacramento Delta. The tract has the quality of being rural but
not, as if it were a museum of a field. We can read it. The Albany
Bulb or landfill is a vestige. Industrial waste waits among
palms and pampas grass. For awhile it is a homeless camp and,
according to the graffiti that remains, a punk pirate paradise.

God & nature
Emotion & narrative

Or the other way around
Without pathos

Or with paths as the Bulb
Filamented with ways through

Crow and gull areas
Of sky dark with violet

Thistles and poppies strangely
Bright white orchards a few

Palms along the edge of dismantled
Farms, dumps, bunkers, dynamite

Plants, homeless-person shanties
And local public art presented in local tones

A songwriter roosts on his farm
Tending flightless creatures

Andrew Bird professional whistler and
Whistler also a professional

have in common the sense of song suggested by their names and
the public success attained by both though both might be said to
have a complicated relationship with his fan base. In Whistler's
case they were mostly women. He said that women were the
future of art. But what did he mean? And he referred to his art
as female, Bird to his birds as clipped of wing. "Go to nature . . .
rejecting nothing, selecting nothing," Ruskin, who was the enemy
of Whistler, said. And so we have gone out to nature taking all of
them, with our fan and peacock feathers in hand, robe knotted,
the morning warm, reading

Rossetti & Poe
Unbeknownst to each other

Are despised, Rossetti by George Inness
For being "like a measure

Worm trying to compass the infinite
Circumference" and Poe

For being a School of Quietudist by Larry Fagin
Referring to Silliman's category of enemies

So Whistler paints his women
And Bird tends his chickens

"in the silent
chicken coop"

Emmanuel Hocquard writes
Relatedly of elegy (see below)

As we might write an elegy
For our enemy when

We can't tell our friends
What we think of them

A semi-Pre-Raphaelite proto-Buddhist sensibility leads them
(with us) to a quest comparable to that of Jack Spicer at his most
linguistic. The *Edinburgh Review* in 1899 suggested that Pre-
Raphaelite women were "tainted at the fountainhead with the
moral and physical unhealth of instincts prematurely developed."
But that is what we want. The quest is for the future. The
exquisite craft and fine coloration attributed to the group is both
admired and despised. Eventually it gives way to a new feeling
which is against the grain, unfinished, subtle, indolent but active

in its indolence, resisting realism by questioning the real, as

"The real sound of the dead." Spicer said
"I have soaked myself in your language."

Not quoted but written. Not above but below. Under, as Silliman's *Under Albany* is not the story of Albany but the story of Silliman. This is that approach. It is not Silliman to whom I refer when I introduce the concept of poison. You know who you are. It is the same lotus and the same mud. Location is everything but is not enough. Nothing is enough. It is the memory of thought troubled by existence. Suspicious of the rich. Resistant of the rest. The refusal to give up is assumed if meaning is what you want in your daily life. To rewrite the laws.

"Here, for a moment, we are joined." [Silliman]
All of time in one place

Surprisingly gentle for a poisonous animal, all nervous system, no brain and yet sophisticated. Like the bulb itself, you are the site of much history.

Of all the sentient beings
I might have saved

Fragile and yet predatory
Why not me? you say

We are friends but I have decided to forget all that. You, like a painter, are more introspective and lyrical or maybe it's me. Your natural moodiness inclines you to paint tonally. The scene is made California-specific by the eucalyptus, the coastline and the background range of lavender hills. That and the roadkill. There is a stable arrangement of horizontal and vertical lines and the color celadon to convey a sense of quiet.

"There is a true country to which we hold
These are its groves, the eucalyptus and the oak,
The cypress and the madrone. These are its fields"

[Robert Duncan, "Ode for Dick Brown"]
[Jack Spicer, "An Arcadia for Dick Brown:"]

"The limiting and stretching mountains of the damned"

The lived and written places are the same in this thinking. The scene and the scenery. To read is to see through each other's texts to the effect of daily light, the golden light that floods the room as I write this morning.

Duncan and Spicer, man and ghost, come together in *An Ode and Arcadia*. Spicer is three years dead, Duncan is almost sixty. The chapbook is published by Ark Press in 1974 but refers to events and work from 1947, when their mutual friend Dick Brown came home from serving time. He had not only refused to be drafted but had also refused to do his time in a CO camp. He walked away from the camp, his hatred for the government requiring that he be sent to prison for defying it, which he was. Brown turned himself in and had a trial, the result of which was three years in the federal penitentiary. Then he came back.

[87]

Cows and clouds
Maze upon maze

William Keith's Tonalist brown
His metallic palette preserved

In the museum of rusted things
George Inness' golden *California*

Harking as it does to the Gilded
[P]age of which we read

When we read *An Ode and Arcadia* we see that it is itself an
occasion, as the writing of the work was an example of the
companion poem. Letters to Kenneth Rexroth are included in
the book. The poems in this Arcadia were submissions to an
anthology of Bay Area poetry that was never published. Rexroth
believed an elegiac tone is what the local writers had in common.

Utilizing what Hocquard later calls
The Robinson Method

In a treatise on elegy
"The island is elegiable" he asserts

"I am the copier of my books . . . "
"And every copier . . . is an islander"

We regret in advance the loss
Of all but the memory of loss

We elegize with anecdote and vocabulary
Taken literally as in "to the letter"

Hocquard insists
In Norma Cole's English

"*This life is mine* means:
This is my list"

Mock, humming, black, blue
And other birds have their say

Here now today reading
Or writing backward in time

Of spring sky or white paper
"a crumpled cow with a crumpled horn

Who lived in the house that Jack built"
Dick, Jack and Robert in Berkeley

The snapshots of the dead
A test for the living

Always fails to remain
In that state In this state

Later in the Mission
In the house owned by Robert and Jess

I come to only after
Robert's death and Jerry's death

Jess and I, both widows,
Don't speak of it and don't

Meet again except in my dreamy and endless
Consideration of his pictures and thinking

About light and other issues
Intrinsic to A Tonalist stance

"When I finally came to the decision to use northern light, the
light in the work became more constant . . . Much of the light in
the Bay Area is diffused and I suppose a little surreal. I think of
Bierstadt when he came out West and did lots of foggy sunsets
and landscapes. They often have a very emotive quality."

[Jess, interview with Michael Auping, *Jess: A Grand Collage, 1951–
1993*]

The bulb is a maze threaded with green where you walk dead west
out to the bay, toward, in fact, into the sea, to the horizon. You
end with light. You soak yourself in my language. It's spring again
and again the new are added to the old dead. "I love you not," as
Rosalind said. "It's a genre problem," she could have gone on.

When a Tonalist depicts Arden
As Albert Pinkam Ryder does

In a painting in front of which having
Just seen the play in Brooklyn

I lose myself because I, like him,
Am a specialist along with Ralph Albert Blakelock

And others in "moonlights," we
Lavish our attentions on the dark light

The simple exchange of atoms
Between friends or among planets

"In windswept SF the light is crystalline sharp when it falls on
objects . . . especially when the luminosity is aslant, it's more
extreme than where I'm from, i.e. East or Midwest, or than
misty Northwest. However I see what you mean when a lot of
sky is in view, like Misrach photos . . . the way the fields smear
light." [Konrad Steiner]

One claims light
The other dark and yet

Seem to be the same
Statement because arranged

As parallel universes do exist
For example yours and mine

Like beams that won't meet
Until space curves or time ends

There is never any time
Even now it seems gone

As we fall bodily from line
To line it is quiet

The sound of my head in your voice
Each word alone with the other

Sounded out as in
I should have told you

Once more from the top
Nothing is what I wanted

10. A Tonalist War

"And why are we fighting, he asked. Because we want
the world, in which our literature belongs, to be freed of
disfigurement." [Peter Weiss, *Aesthetics of Resistance*]

But who is out there
Birding the sun?

And what is left?
A long morning followed

By a long night
The linear battlefield of yesterday

A list of the dead vexes
The president's vacation

Like meteorology he is in the prediction business
But when did you realize you could be a lucid dreamer?

The skin white as marble
Or the marbleized sky means

Rain sometimes
A catastrophe or no rain

Or the earth is the weather
History is the same

When a war is fought between Turkey and Russia, France enters
and then England, calling it the Crimean War. Until recently, it
was known as history's most unnecessary war. The generals who
were to fight the Civil War in the U.S. visited the Crimea to
learn about the modern battlefield. Marx reported on it for the
Times. Marbles were being excavated then in Turkey, according
to Peter Weiss, but their removal was not affected by the war.

After the war the Arts and Crafts movement
Begins in England and finds an ideal home

In California's *Philopolis*
As William and Lucia Matthews

Called their magazine
Or later in *Semina*, a California

Or two ago, Wallace Berman
Replaces paradise with itself

A cataclysm of natural and historical forces occurs. We don't
feel it until we do. One by one our lives are changed or saved or
lost. Catastrophes increase in frequency until there is one every
day and then one every hour. "Are you prepared for disaster?"
the supermarket loudspeaker asks when I am in San Diego. The
firestorm season comes and the border burns. No one is ready
when something burns.

When the weather kills
We are reminded by death

That death is natural
Displacement everyday

Anguish ordinary and
Inevitable the word

Compassion comes up
Capacity also

Many writers are cultural workers. Others work for causes
as fundraisers or administrators. Others for businesses or
institutions that provide a variety of products, as books, that can
be used to resist the powers that, however, ultimately control the
businesses in question, if not the products themselves. Who has
this control? How can it be demonstrated? Or can we stipulate
that the control exists and that it is inimical to anyone whose
class affiliation is lower than upper? Do we think that these
activities matter because someone, somewhere (perhaps it is
ourselves), can get access to something that would otherwise
remain hidden or invisible? Tell a story here. Show that the work
of making the invisible visible is endless, that a new version is
constantly required.

Can you stray from your class?
Or does language itself determine

Your intentions? What are
Your intentions?

Does the fact that *The Daily Compromise*
Was founded in 2000 mean

That nothing can be done?
I can prove the opposite proposition

With any of your lines
"Working notes handed out." [Taylor Brady]

"Gutenberg is watching" [Alan Halsey]

"A shred of cloud totally profiling
bruise." [Alli Warren]

"Your mistrust, fellow citizens, is natural." [Brent
Cunningham]

Reaching for the books that are to hand
You find a familiar lexicon but belief

Where do you find that?
Is the bruise visible?

Is it legible? They meet in a room to discuss art while the
war goes on. Some people die every day. There are automated
phone calls. They sound real. Art is the thing they do. The
people in this room. Glamour means everything to them and
they would die, glamorously, to bring about what they felt was
fundamental change. Others quietly persist. Still others, not in
the room, feel that if they can convince us that people, enemies

of freedom, also not in the room, are trying to kill us, we will allow them to do anything. Let's call them the government. These would-be killers identify the U.S. with the government. They say there is no difference between us and it. Thinking of them with compassion is not the same as doing nothing.

The silence of the afternoon air
In this grove is expensive

However you look at it you
Don't usually see it from the chair

At your desk where the question is
Can you comprehend

The whole set-up while you are
Implicated in its outcome?

The real weather is the war
We are all in

We can't stop them
As in arrest is to cause

To rest but there is no
Time for that we say stop

But should we simply
Stop having begun?

When will it be time to go, if not now?
The religious people will take over

As they have done here
Making it illegal not to answer

About yourself under
The Patriot Act even if

As a patriot you consider it
Your duty not to answer

The Dalai Lama speaks about compassion. He says it's too early
to decide about the war. What is he thinking? Perhaps about
the loss of his country to the invasion by China. The world let it
happen. We are the world. The statues were broken. The marble
ground down like bones.

Deadly asymmetrical events
Precede visits by uniformed

Messengers dreaded
By those who wait

Those who go don't
Want to go but are

Overtaken by events
And the consequences of not

Going so they go
Fathers and or gang members

According to Sean Labrador
Whose father as mine

Went to war
But what are we doing now?

What is the genre of this activity? Is it a street fight, a
humanitarian rescue, a diplomatic mission or all three
simultaneously and by turns? Unpredictable and sudden, things
change from one to the other. The term Three Block Warfare
can refer to these actions or to the three city blocks in which
they often occur. Network Centric Warfare is another term,
meaning the use of knowledge processing in battle as well as
the synchronizing and swarming of small groups in an unstable
environment of intense conflict. Decisions are made there by
individuals whose training is brief, whose knowledge is limited
and whose central motive is to stay out of the line of fire.

By means of fire
For which there are special names

At different times "We don't do a lot of
Hearts and minds here it's irrelevant"

Amateurs talk about theory
Professionals about logistics

How to get it done? As in any job, it's the same thing over and over. How to move things from here to there. Wait for the election to fight the battle. Stuff happens. My enemy's enemies are my friends. Religious fundamentalists from the U.S. and Iran in cahoots with each other. This is what Iraqis believe according to the Baghdad Burning blogger. What does she know?

White phosphorus is Whiskey Pete
Made from pee by alchemists

In the 17th century "It was
17th century tactics," a soldier says

Of Fallujah, "It's under siege"
As fury fantasizes or vigilance resolves

Marines, Iraqi security and commandos
Begin "debriding Fallujah of its guerrillas"

According to *Time*
It is called the cold light

It burns through the person leaving the clothes intact. It is not cold. They were seeking the philosopher's stone. It is conventional to burn people during a war. They always mention the bones. It burns to the bones.

Lies, fire, things that explode
Deployed conventionally

Poetic as weapon
"against logical analysis" [Alan Halsey]

Synthesizes "sense, shape & sound" so that the words are the
event and the event is not explicable and can't be paraphrased.
Nothing is the same. History is yesterday.

"Standing there lost in memory I started to hear the skeletal
scrape of leaves bouncing along the driveway. For a second I
caught a familiar scent on the wind, the smoky tang of seasoned
wood crackling on a fire. That phantom smell was enough to
soften the cold lines of the forward operating base, and the next
breath I took pushed me even farther into memory. For a few
minutes . . . I was home . . . Until I was once again standing on
an ugly roof. In Baghdad. Alone."

[Danjel Bout, *365 and a Wakeup*, blog]

The afternoon panic is silent, is the poem
"More accurate than any report"?

What is the worst you have seen?
He asks his father on the way to Iraq

There is a huge book called *The Torture Papers*
He is a plastic surgeon

I can't repeat the story, he says
It dreams about the war

11. The Romantic Future

When do I write? you ask
In the morning and again

At night when do you write?
Is the light involved at all

Or time as I have time we say
To right something or is nothing

Made to stand again by this action?
And is it the same nothing

You know when you have written or
When you listen

Does the action stand for
A new you or new year

More abstract and younger than I
Or you appear as if

I were a man and you
A question posed between us

Were the weeds, flowers and low scrub
Of the bulb how would we

Write or would the words
Written or blood spilled

Rewrite the lines in our palms
Changing the present into something

We don't believe in like Romantic Futurism
Or the palms and pampas grass

Of the punk pirate paradise
Going out into the bay

Articulated earlier as being
The state one is in when

Present in this geography
From the beginning Gottardo

Piazonni, Tonalist, was in touch
With F. T. Marinetti, Futurist

But chose to paint the plaster pillars
Of California and the moons

In his head made plain though
Flatly we are not there but here

At the corner of the table with the poets in a painting by Fantin-Latour, one of the Société de Trois as he, Legros and Whistler called themselves. "Whistler, American," as Pound bragged. Rimbaud and Verlaine are in the picture (it is an homage to Baudelaire). The postcard is pale from hanging in the sun in our living room until you died and I moved out. It is visible also in a photo of Wallace Berman in *Semina Culture*, iconographic for an extended generation of writers and artists. One poet in the picture appears to be wearing the characteristic down jacket of the seventies. Rimbaud looks out. Verlaine is in love, his forehead like a moon above his face. I see us in disguise or it's our fate I see.

Whistler as Pan by Beardsley
Also called *Enigmatic Love*

The eight or five or three who formed a like-minded group of artists banding together to generate sales was not seen at the time as a movement and can only be seen now as the imaginary community that it was. Unsatisfied personal desires and professional ambition were nothing to the nonconformist ideals and despair that characterized their lives. Here is Whistler draped over an expensive chair in his exquisite bohemian costume. We picture him together. Or you alone. "I have no time for the possibilities of success," Duncan wrote. "Each fulfillment precludes it."

Snapping out of it
The room fills with air
Where we are present
It starts up again

This never being lucky
Except when we are

It is the one day of the year when we meet in the plaza of the little
hill around the corner from the gun shop. Did I tell you I am from
the country you are currently idealizing? It is busy here in the café.
I remember what you will say in advance about the surface of the
real. I started with the cards long ago.

They are virtual now
Like yourself at this moment

An egret fills the window
Of the sky with wings

An older lady with patterns
An umbrella with rain

That is me she says of the weather
The reader finds her place on the screen

When letters are exchanged
What happens is electric

The rain collects
The reader is also a collection

She thinks of you
When she thinks of me

Let him stand for anything
She says Let him go on

12. Long time no

You are home
When you read

This a new
Element appears

Californium or
Ether either

Explodes or
You are glad to see me

Barely audible or at times loud. Complaints and admissions
side by side with whatever else you've got. A small house in the
woods. Tiny sun. Tiny moon. Or nothing but fog and beyond
that the world.

And stooges
Three

The summer dry
Climate we

Had when we had
A climate

Before the war
The sea the hills the

Children
A beach book

I read backward
To the source

Of the river mouth
Thicket to ticket

Where you arrive
To write

"With a taste for boundlessness and in a mood for annihilation"
Bermuda Antigua, Standard Schaefer

Not you and
Then yes you your

Version
Since unwritten

Vision
Recomposition

As of relatives (mine)
Hung for stealing bread

Unsung
Antiheroic

Island dwellers
Not in your mind

In my heart I read what you want to hide. I forget it. It forgets
me. We get together in a party or a movement moving heaven and
earth until only earth is left. Or heaven. These are the last pages
of the notebook. Your mind is mine, you say, not romantically but
as a category shift, or maybe this is a con. I give A Tonalist talk.
I start with the letter and work my way to the space between.
Words. I am there now. I go back and forth until I get to the next
letter. It is a correspondence. And then there is the sound of the
song. A tonality embraced by the reader when the writer escapes.
And vice versa. Emptiness. Space. Whatever you want to call it.
It is left to its own devices. Finally a person appears. A reference
or referent. Client, patron or customer. She is alive in the act of
reading. Actual size. Fat chance. Ample even.

It. It.
Again   .

I live in the work of my friends, she says, and I wonder if this
means she feels most alive when she is reading. She says yes and
no, mostly no, mentioning her husband, her lover and her kid.
I say me too and we sit for a minute picturing the friends, the
husbands, etc.

I feel implicated
By the suggestion

Of there being
A fourth stooge

See below
Start over

These are almost poems. That we write at all is subject to doubt.
Doom. Direct and then not. Nothing to be said but yes to it.

"Don't
watch the moon. Do something."

[*Imitation Poems*
Patrick Durgin]

"For him, each apposite
sonority was etiological"

"My Human"
And later

"free of psychology at last untrue
here's my signature it's"

Legal then. Signed. What a relief! There is agreement. It is
personal, realistic, accurate, available and untrue.

Works for me
But for you

What will work? Where will you go when it's over? Where have
you already gone? It's more like a TV series than a geography.
You complain. You send another ticket, another picture of the
bottom of the cell floor. Of your sea I sing, you say anthemically
and I say I don't believe you, but don't I

Reason as in
Resonate

Love as in
"Love ate"

The take includes pictures
I celebrate

The real I see
She begins again

To sing of thee
As if the past

Caught existing
Works for me she repeats

"The bright light of remainder."
(remains) Melissa Buzzeo

What Began Us
And to what end?

And when
Can I see you?

Beloved. Reader. Which is it? Someone says he is against the next
war. Not me you say. I won't go. Have already not gone. It is not
a war or a metaphor but a convention — a convening. We look for
it. It finds us cohering loosely, a fact or a faction. Is this a war or
a police action? Is this that? Can't get no. You made me take that
line out before but here it is again. The world.

Your next book
The war over

Your topia
Don't get me started

"Art, or situations of partially suspended disbelief, of
foregrounding, of heightening or intentional flattening, of
protected description and inflated proposition, is a locus, in any
society at any scale, for strategic relations as a kind of model."

Mike Scharf
For Kid Rock/Total Freedom

So is this a novel or a prophecy? Idly fingering the trigger. What
will I say when someone asks after you? What have I already said?

The reading tonight
The dead. The undead.

Children who are vampires
Lovers who are Martians

Redefined
We march

Raggedly
The tune

In the wrong time. Oneself not in one's right mind. By meaning
overcome. By rights done. By nights undone. But someone wants
your music.

A reader stops by
Asking the writer

About the deal
The dealer replies

By dealing
The next thing

You here or not. Present but unrequited. Unseated. Unsighted.
Collectively. *non* is not a category but a pretext. Collaborative in
the worst sense. Feeding off each other in a frenzy. Your teeth. My
dark thoughts. The horizon. Those in the bay are counted. Sharks
not poets. Together for a time. Solitary hunters at the top of the
food chain look down on us in our bright schools.

Emergent
Sublunary

Not the moon
By definition

Not a geography
But telemetric

"We exist
amid permanent damage to the replica." [Estrin]

Long an illusion
The world ends

The Northwest Passage
Stops not being

Hell not frozen though over
Heaven cold

"Sing my astronaut suit"
Estrin again

Snow Sensitive Skin
Brady and Halpern

"descending into recon by fire"

Where Shadows Will

for Norma, again when

Full night but bright
Scans wide
Pans back
Often rarely we
As now at table or
Together in our heads try
Not to hide
We don't die

Until a long time later. We meet. I read your book. Each new
line. I get lost in the familiar words. It's win win or lose lose.
This is the last contradiction. As if I had control over that.
Over these. Aloud. Now. Here. There. You declare.

"Not to be seen is to be dead"
But I say
This death is in your head
It's my turn to pay and you
That I already
And why not
Have paid

Or will see
A shadow where

Space left
Everything out

When the negative
A positive for
Another
Taken literally not

For granted
Yours or mine also not
You alive now my love
And I know

A Tonalist Coda

"Table manners are useless if there's nothing to eat. Poetry has to
have passion for its food—either passion cooked up in tranquility or
tranquility cooked up in passion. Eastern "poetry" has neither. We
wait politely at the table and are served nothing but silverware."

Jack Spicer, from "Dialogue of Eastern and Western Poetry"

1. Some History

When, at a recent event, I first heard of a dialogue written on
index cards by Jack Spicer and Robin Blaser with commentary by
Robert Duncan, I was intrigued. I knew of Spicer's determination
to keep his poetry in the West Coast, even specifically in San
Francisco, of Duncan's complex relationship with publication and
of Blaser's decamping for a Canadian West Coast presumably even
more distant from the East than the Bay Area. Because the poetics
of this circle of friends informs my own practice and that of the
writers whose work I have thought of as A Tonalist, without their
permission, engagement and occasionally without their knowledge,
I wondered if these index cards would have anything to do with
my thinking about A Tonalist and my intention to write about it
here.

When I read the text (published in Miriam Nichols' *Even On
Sunday: Essays, Readings and Archival Materials on the Poetry and
Poetics of Robin Blaser*), I initially thought there was little that

related to my sense of A Tonalist. This written conversation took place in 1956, when Spicer and Blaser were about thirty, Duncan a bit older. The cards were long part of Robert Duncan's papers at the Bancroft Library at UC Berkeley but only when Kevin Killian and Peter Gizzi discovered one card that had been separated from the bunch in a new set of Spicer's papers did the whole set of them see the light of day.

In this exchange, Spicer asserts a Western (West Coast) poetics by resisting what he believes to be an Eastern (East Coast) dominant poetics. The dialogue begins with Spicer: "Eastern poetry — there isn't any Eastern poetry — and besides, too many people read it." So the dominance is stated here as a readership monopoly. Eastern poetry is taking up too much of the mental real estate that Spicer imagines to be allotted to poetry. Duncan and Blaser question Spicer's sense of Eastern poetry, pointing out that many poets who would fall under the "Eastern" category actually live in the West and vice versa. Duncan and Blaser each also then ascribe value to poets they assume Spicer would term Eastern and whose poetics they don't share but seem to respect. Spicer eschews such civility. His counter arguments are more passionate than logical and he seems gleefully aware of it, as for example in this response to several assertions by Blaser and Duncan that there might be some value in reading "Eastern poets:" "There's not one under forty that does anything. They just rhyme and pick their noses." As Kevin points out in the essay that accompanied the publication of the piece, the writing on these index cards, is an effort to reproduce the vivacity of table talk. The project falls slightly flat, but is interesting in the context of what other texts show to exist at this point in their poetics and for what follows both in their friendship and in their other work.

On closer consideration I realized that, in several ways, I had found exactly what I was looking for in this exchange, both as historical information about the roots of A Tonalist and as a good example of what A Tonalist is exactly *not* about. In this conversation, Spicer asserts a group identity, shared by his interlocutors who, in turn and in spite of their concurrence with the poetics proposed by Spicer, point out the contradictions generated by any such assertion. Duncan refers to the kind of work they value as Vitalist, an interesting name for the writing he values, but one that clearly didn't last. From a contemporary perspective, I see the term as an interesting alternative to "experimental."

As I reread it, their argument finally began to seem useful to me, even emblematic, partly because of the connection between Spicer/Duncan/Blaser poetics and those of A Tonalist, but also because it is group formation in action. Spicer's assertion against table manners without sustenance can be read as a diatribe against craft or technique for its own sake and against work that aims to fulfill expectations rather than outraging them or that is written to be part of literature (part of the curriculum) rather than to be something that will not easily fit into the canon. There is a lot to hate there, but Spicer was a great hater and, while A Tonalist may take exception to some of his objections, we are sympathetic. But of greater interest is how, in this exchange, one can watch group formation include contradictions, inconsistencies, refutations and assertions, as well as personal relationships that, importantly, often form the basis of all else.

A Tonalist is not a style but an attitude or perhaps a context. It is not a set of techniques. The surface(s) of work that might be called A Tonalist are not superficially similar. A Tonalist proposes an anti-lyric whose viability relates to the history of lyric poetry by resisting as much as enacting it. The table manners are bad. The tranquility being cooked up comes from emptiness. And passion, as everyone knows, means suffering. In *A Tonalist* the lyric "I" is complicated rather than celebrated. There is doubt. There is, as Kafka said, hope, but not for us. Perhaps that is a lot to ask of a poetics — that it write itself right out of or up against the canon or the idea of literature, that it shoot itself in the foot. The sense of dissatisfaction or self-destruction, not with the person but with the writing subject, is rife.

Such a poetics need not, in fact does not, have a location. Back in the day, however, Jack Spicer loved to assert California as being important to his poetics, to his group and to his enterprise as a writer. Famously he refused to allow his work to be published outside of the Bay Area. I don't share this orientation, which seems part consciously mad poetic jingoism and partly sour grapes, but the locations he often celebrated are the ones I have lived in for most of my life. I have often walked in his mental and actual footprints. However, the idea that place influences the writing of a group of people who are intensely connected to each other and to it, interested me when me when I began writing A Tonalist and continues to be a notion, perhaps a legend.

The only place directly associated with A Tonalist is a blog called A Tonalist Notes which, like any group blog, includes individuals from a number of locations and has readers from all around. This nonplace follows an earlier site called *non* that was A Tonalist before I had invented the term (like much else mentioned here).

The effect of place is not easily discerned. Perhaps those who are attracted to a place and then stay there to make and take part in the milieu have some things in common with it and themselves. For example, is there a heritage among New York City writers of New York School thinking and writing — use of lists, speech, other elements? I feel if we were in a bar together I could convince you that there is. The notion that a poetics can be connected to a place is always difficult to prove, even if, as in this case of New York School, it might seem apparent.

The Bay Area attributes I have identified from Spicer's time that seem to me to relate to A Tonalist today are a sense of elegy and of utopianism (or more usually dystopianism). Elegy was claimed by Kenneth Rexroth and others as being characteristic of the Bay Area in particular. In his book, *San Francisco Renaissance*, Michael Davidson quotes Duncan's letter to Rexroth agreeing that elegy is the thing that could connect such different poets as himself and William Everson. Rexroth planned to make a Bay Area anthology with the idea of elegy in mind but he never did. Many, including Richard Candida Smith in his *Utopia and Dissent: Art, Poetry and Politics in California*, have noted the utopianism here. For example, the painter Jay DeFeo, a contemporary of Spicer, Duncan and Blaser, refused to attend Dorothy Miller's prestigious Sixteen Americans show in New York, though the inclusion of her work in it was both an honor and a potentially important moment in her career. This was a gesture of Bay Area hubris that would have warmed Spicer's heart had he known of it.

But that was then. A Tonalist is not about place, not limited to a particular place but, like the Duncan/Spicer circle and others before it, A Tonalist is made of, found among, an extended group of people who share an acquaintance. They sometimes have a connection to the Bay Area (and to me) but it might be tenuous. As a young art student I was told that Bay Area painters differed from their New York counterparts in that they were more figurative, more attached to the human form. It was a commonplace of the time. When later I became aware of a questioning of lyric practice in the poetry community of the 80s, I felt that my own attention to lyric, despite the resistance to an unquestioned celebration of voice, craft and bourgeois beauty among other resistances I shared with its detractors, constituted a parallel gesture with that old figurative impulse. The desire to retain the possibilities of lyric was something that I shared most intensely with Jerry Estrin and later with Norma Cole. Some people write lyric poetry because they just want to and think it is great. Some write it though they think it is impossible. The latter are A Tonalists.

On a visit to New York in 2003 I read with Pamela Lu at the Bowery Poetry Club. That reading was, I believe, my first from *A Tonalist*, which, at the time, I think I was still calling *Tonalism*. At a restaurant afterwards, I commented that there was, in old Tonalist landscapes, a quality of California light that seemed familiar to me and that I wished to get to in what I was writing. Pam Lu was interested and immediately wanted me to say more about what I could mean by that. I did but felt she was unsatisfied with my answer. Let me try again. Tonalism interested me from the moment I first heard of it in art history classes or maybe I just saw it as an intriguing footnote in the required reading. It is a kind of landscape painting in which the technique is dark and there is emphasis on a mysterious or even a spiritual quality. Though it seems anti-modernist the painters who identified that way or took up the style were very much aware of what was going on in the art world. Some painted Impressionist paintings along with their Tonalist efforts. Some didn't use the word in relation to their work but were later included in Tonalist exhibitions. One such show occurred in 1995 at the Oakland Museum. It was called *Twilight and Reverie*. The phrase says a lot. What appealed to me about Tonalism was not only the dark intimate landscapes of local scenes but my perception that it was an orientation irresistibly taken up by people who could have gone to (or stayed in) Paris and become one of the ten thousand Impressionists said to have been there at the time. They knew better and did it anyway. Xavier Martinez went to Paris to study, made a success of it and then left a promising continental career to return to San Francisco. Tonalism was local and yet national. Part of its influence is from the 19th century Barbizon school in France and it has been associated with the work of James Abbott McNeill Whistler and yet it is, like Whistler, American. The paintings, by Martinez, Gottardo Piazzoni and others, look to me like the old California I still see around me. This Bohemian California was in a dialog with the European art world in a way that was knowledgeable yet provincial. The local utopianism took on an ancient Greek form that set the stage for Isadora Duncan, as well as for Robert Duncan. There is a connection between Tonalism and my sense of A Tonalist, but the writers whose work I find to be A Tonalist would probably find that they had little interest in that old style of painting, though I might be able to make a case for why it connects.

Obsessing more about my exchange with Pam Lu, I realize that the *Ambient Parking Lot* atmosphere of the South Bay, so accurately evoked by her own prose of that title, works for me as a modern equivalent of a particularly Cailfornian landscape. Her approach avoids the prettiness of those old paintings, but Pam Lu's Bay Area is not the one of Piazzoni's pillars or Arthur and Lucia Matthews' Isadora-like dancing girls. Her description is deadpan. It sometimes is the content. Foreground and background blend. There are shadows. This brings up the connected point that A Tonalist can be prose. In fact, much of the poem *A Tonalist* is essay or memoir. Much of my own current writing (including this?) is fiction. A Tonalist prose seeks to complicate while it explicates but in a useful, even a utilitarian, way. Pam Lu's own words, from an excerpt of *The Second to Last Country,* published in a chapbook by A Rest Press on the occasion of our reading, are a good example of a prose redolent of the particular magic of the South Bay

> How can I possibly express, that which is nearly impossible to locate in human expression, namely, the terrible fondness and affection I feel for the sights, sounds, smells, tastes and textures of my favorite sit-down diner chain, or the specific ache I experience upon recognizing the perpendicular dark blue street signs with white gothic lettering that mark the arteries of certain friendly and welcoming subdivision housing tracts?

Pam goes on, in this excerpt, to point out that such imperial architecture is "infinitely portable" and can be found "anywhere in the world." It's not that she is describing California here, though she probably is, or that she is making a landscape, but the tense, emotive frame of her observation makes this text seem A Tonalist to me. The value placed on what is not usually valued despite or even because of the awareness of negative qualities in this phenomenon, this form, this expression of modern life is not totally unlike the relationship I would expect an A Tonalist to have with lyric or with having a writing practice at all. It is the quality of "despite." An atmosphere of doubt, honesty and awareness of all the drawbacks exists within the context of a determination (that is also strangely pleasure-driven) to go there anyway.

Here it seems appropriate to mention Jen Hofer and Patrick Durgin, formerly of the Bay Area (Jen was born here), but currently located in LA and Chicago. In their collaborative book, *The Route*, they have cultivated a way of thinking about (among a number of other things) place, displacement and the exchanges that are possible among people — themselves, their correspondents and interlocutors — who have poetics and affection in common but not location. There is self-consciousness in *The Route* of not being written in a particular location (or a particular genre) but locating the work in a place that is always literally on the way. They write, in a letter to me, of the conventions of correspondence found in my own *Self-Destruction* and the ramifications of taking the possibilities of their exchange to heart:

> We've been thinking about a way that locations intuit themselves into being when actual geographic distance is sustained. But what if that distance is unverifiable? . . . What kind of knowing is insinuated in the discursive address of

epistles? And of whom? So this is how we find ourselves
reading the "Convention" poems, although they are clearly
implicated in a lyric, maybe a tonalist enterprise as well as an
epistolary one.

Jen Hofer and Patrick Durgin, *The Route*

Like Spicer, Jen and Patrick use letters to each other and others to
find the route. The route here consists of finding a way to move
forward in writing that honors the doubts, resistances, provisos,
rules and illusions these two writers have accumulated from
Iowa, Buffalo, the Bay Area, Mexico, Minnesota, Chicago and
many points in between, including a lot of reading and arguing
and a massive amount of real life. Their nexus of relationships is
international and multi-genre. It is inclusive, personal and timely.

Like the atopia, if I can call it that, created by Jen and Patrick in
their book and unlike the "West Coast" poetics asserted by Spicer
in the index card conversation, A Tonalist is not defined by hatred
of other poets or groups. It does not seek to disclude but values
contradiction and compromise. The word bastardization occurs to
me — to be declared fatherless and without legitimacy. To be of
irregular or dubious origin, not genuine — to be no better than
one should be, to have a dubious future and the air of being part
of and yet separate from the situation. Is that A Tonalist? Am
I the only A Tonalist or can the word be usefully applied to or
appropriated by others? If it is useful, it is because the writing and
writers in question, question. They are permeable to, by and in the
context of others.

Here I want to bring up the poetry map I once found at the American Poetry Archives when I first went to work there. The Archives is part of the Poetry Center at SF State and is comprised almost entirely of sound and moving images of poets reading. There isn't really a map or diagram collection, but nevertheless I found this map, apparently drawn by past archives workers and reflecting a distinctly 70s and early 80s view of the Bay Area poetry world. As I recall, there was nothing surprising to me in it. I had more or less the same map in my head. Language poetry was there, along with New Narrative and I think the Kearny Street workshop poets, the Women's Writers Union, Beats, of course, Bolinas people and many other varieties of writers and writing. Since then, that imagined map has changed and changed again. Map technology itself is not what it was. The most basic terms of the relationship between writer and reader are in flux. Is A Tonalist anti-lyric poetry written in a way that questions the very fact of its being poetry and attempts to break down the self while attempting also to assist the threatened person? Spicer again: "The self is no longer real." Is that (this) a manifesto or just another false proposition?

2. Some Presences

One's intimate community of interlocutors changes a lot over one's lifetime. There are many writers who have remained central to my own thinking and then there are the writers and other artists who are central to their thinking. It's like a phone tree. I have hesitated in this essay to implicate Norma Cole in the formation of A Tonalist. When I first thought up A Tonalist partly in response

to my own feelings about the stroke she suffered in 2002, I asked
Norma a question — something like did it make sense to speak
of our work in that way. In some way, the question was a way
to focus on what we did together. We were close, traveling and
experiencing holidays and big events. Norma was with me when
Jerry Estrin died. It was she who closed his eyes. At the time of
my proposing A Tonalist, she was still in the hospital. I have written
before about the incident and recently Robin Tremblay-McGraw,
in an interview in XPoetics, asked Norma to characterize the
agreement, the "yes" I have claimed. Norma responded

> My "yes" then meant I could muse about something that was
> not involved with my having a stroke. I was in the hospital,
> couldn't talk, walk or use the right side of my body. It was
> such a relief to see Laura, hear what she was thinking about
> — and I am always interested in the armatures people think
> about or towards.

> I had been involved with thinking about Schoenberg,
> listening to his work. Reading about Schoenberg's "Pierrot
> Lunaire," and also about the Committee of Mothers of
> Russian Soldiers, I then wrote a little "song," a passacaglia to/
> for both:

> I saw shells . . .
> . . . that were bigger than I was."
> Journalist, Chechnya, 8 March, 1995
> Rhythms are precise, the
> intervals approximate

Night, passacaglia
black butterflies
in front of the sun
killing memory

Night is scored for
Soldiers mothers
Come in trains to take
Them home

Worldstruck, with an instrument
Night, gift and theft

**(Contrafact, 1996).

Possibly it's an "a tonalist" poem avant la lettre.

Exactly. Norma's response characterizes most A Tonalist practice
at this point and probably forever because anyone who is A
Tonalist would share Norma's resistance to being limited to being
in a group. It is also appropriate that she mentions Schoenberg
because atonalism with its connection to John Cage was also
important to me as a writer and is part of why I adopted the term.
The reference to music (and to *Silence*) in the " tone" part of A
Tonalist emphasizes the existence of tone in multiple disciplines.
Tone suggests musicality and can also relate to accent, emphasis,
force, inflection, intonation, resonance and a range of color terms
such as hue, shade, tinge, tint and value. When "A" is added you
have of all of the above, but separated as you are by an eternal gap,
you are left with a quality of being astringent, flat, dystopian.

Cage's comments on and practice of art in *Silence* and *A Year From Monday* dazzled me as a young poet in the 70s. The way the text includes both commentary and examples of work and yet also stands to one side of the fact of Cage's practice which was, after all, music, was completely enabling and entirely confusing to me. I felt his books were meant to be workbooks of a way of living. Not a blueprint but, as with Spicer, a set of propositions or admonitions.

I wrote "A Tonalist Rules" early in the life of the blog, A Tonalist Notes. Both the poem and the blog were a way to provide and cultivate responses to imaginary and actual questions about what A Tonalist was. The poem is actually a part of a collection of pieces called *Divination*, valuing as it does the gamesmanship and sense of risk that characterize the pieces in that book.

A tonalist rules

For the game
When we are unafraid
Narrative coincides with meaning
Flatly in love with
Rhetorical continuity interrupted
Only to be taken back up
Like two things in one
Beauty for example
The present and past enter into
A prosody of unfinished gesture
Against formal predictability
Synopsis is predicament

Irony mitigated by shamelessness
Lack of value for the conspicuous
Turning mentioned earlier
Of fate into history
Unable to be made
Unfashionable as the fact
Of particularity
When prediction becomes
Love of that
Chance

In response to the poem and a lot of discussion at Small Press
Distribution where Brent Cunningham and I have worked
together for ten years, he has commented, in the A Tonalist
blog, "I am A tonalist, not the tonalist, problematically neither
untonal or tonal." He goes on to write,

> Grounded in situational practice: that is, there are no
> a priori determinations regarding specific use of style,
> technique, form, order. Importantly, this is not a lack of
> aesthetic theory. In a sense it is theory theorizing upon
> theory. The indeterminate is never, here, transcendentally
> indeterminate: rather it maintains a connection to the
> determinate of its being claimed in the first place. Just as
> the unknowable is only and merely something a person may
> come to know, this indeterminate is something that may
> very well be tethered to a forthcoming determination.
> So this non-declaration of the A tonalist, however wavery, is
> hence meaningful.

This was a time of much amusing ranting among us at work, in emails, at readings and elsewhere. I became aware that Standard Schaefer was interested in the possibilities of argument present in A Tonalist. Standard's musicality and awareness of politics along with an almost *noir* sense of negativity, caused him to relate easily to the A Tonalist ideas being put forward then. In relation to Brent's post and to my poem he wrote

> On the micro-level, to be an A Tonalist might mean to carve out a space where many small gestures, musicalities, and coincidences can be legitimated within your own work . . . Or maybe it produces thought or vision but not knowledge or certainty. There is no shared style and no efforts to legitimate the differences and similarities between us.

> On the molar level, there are perhaps affinities within the various works and writers that cannot represent A Tonalism. There is no reason to represent it. If I come out of or work in a tradition that is against representation, I might seriously consider myself unrepresentable.

Sometimes I am on the verge of thinking A Tonalist entirely a fiction. Then I find that a younger writer has produced a text or made a gesture that I recognize as entirely A Tonalist and then I again think that the kind of writing or writer that I think of as A Tonalist exists. This always seems amazing to me. Because I am now working in fiction I am aware that the idea of A Tonalist is like a fiction imposed on reality. In my life, it is a strangely affectionate, intimate term that serves as a point of agreement and understanding among friends — when it is mentioned, which is almost never.

An important influence on and source of A Tonalist thinking, the English writer Alan Halsey brings into the A Tonalist mix a group of writers he has published and drunk with for the last few decades. Alan's prodigious output as a writer, visual artist and publisher enlivens this English pod of A Tonalist activity which includes the work of Geraldine Monk and other individuals who, in Alan's work, are occasionally identified as Logoclasts. There is a parallel between the idea of A Tonalist and Logoclast which can both be defined as comprising readers (writers) who arrive at either of the terms and, feeling both relieved and revealed, agree to them, before simply going on. Alan took the word from Gregory Vincent St Thomasino's *Logoclosody Manifesto* in which St Thomasino comments, enigmatically, "The mind knows the word in the figure of its substance." St Thomasino includes Alan Halsey's work in a short list of Logoclast phenomena. Alan's use of the term in his writing is evocative because it seems to refer to his use of synonyms, antonyms and other Logoclastic moves to amuse the reader while focusing attention on the surface of the language in a way that belies the interesting points being made. Like many, these A Tonalists don't, as far as I know, regard themselves as such.

Alan's "On Poetic," (written between 1980 and 1982) appeared in the A Tonalist Notes blog in 2006. As it was written long before the time of A Tonalist, it is clearly, to use Norma's term, "a tonalist, *avant la lettre.*" "On Poetic" is more (hypnotic?) suggestion than manifesto. Beginning with the use of the word "Poetic" rather than "Poetics," these directives articulate a way of thinking that reduces to the essential. Alan suggests and demonstrates that concision in language can work toward a satisfying compression of thought. The last of these fifteen suggestions, or dicta, on poetic, characteristically invokes the broad concept of "Imagination," then connects it to specific actions in language and, of course, in doing this it presents itself as an example of the desired outcome.

> Thought at the maximum degree — Imagination, in Blake's sense, the opposite of Fancy. And this comes down to the merest technicalities: e.g. the rightful precedence of noun over adjective — that adjectives are the tools of Fancy, their abundance a blur — whereas poetic risks with its precision the rough-edge of meaning, turns that pressure on the word: appears to pass into nonsense and pass back. In-turns, and proceeds out of language; creating what it means; meaning just what it creates.

"On Poetic" suggests not a style or technique but criteria, a working model or set of admonitions, not, as with Spicer, against God. Rather these recommendations are *for* finding the poem entirely within the logic (the logos) of the words in it. It seems necessary here to include an earlier admonition — for me this is the most A Tonalist moment in "On Poetic" — to remind us what the compression invoked is not about:

> The demand for precision is too easily presented as reductive, a mere paring-down. 'One thing at a time' — whereas poetic always says two-things-at-once.

A Tonalist might add meanings beyond two and, if these impacted meanings create difficulty, if you laugh at them instead of with them, so much the better. It is typical of A Tonalist to see the humor in the line or situation and take it seriously (or not) anyway. This kind of behavior in a poem relates to the "Irony mitigated by shamelessness" mentioned above. As Alan points out in his most recent book, *Term as in Aftermath*, in an eponymously titled poem which begins "THEMPYRE. The literal said it. No use" — "Satire will always be your friend."

Occasionally I notice that younger writers mention A Tonalist, usually in relation to me but occasionally to refer to a gesture in writing that might also be called anti-lyric. "Anti-lyric" much as with "A Tonalist," can be thought of as a gesture in poetry that includes the thing it is resisting. Before or, it must be, during the writing of *The Route*, Patrick participated in A Tonalist Notes, posting in response to my blogging about his earlier book *Color Music*. This work of Patrick's was for me foundational to my idea of A Tonalist, allowing me to know for sure that A Tonalist was not just me and friends in my generation of writers but was identifiable in new work. *Color Music* wasn't written as an A Tonalist text, as by definition it is not actually possible to do that, but was composed as a way to figure out what to do next. Well after the book was written and published, Patrick wrote in the A Tonalist Notes blog:

> I become a tonalist on my lunch hour today. Thank you for having me.

> But, dear Martian, what I do is to make things, and this making is not about new things made but about the process and its desires in achieving appositives, whose plurality

entails alienating devices as much as synthesis. In other words, the music is the desire for song which is somewhat unresolved or at least infinitely mutable — i.e., any sound I can produce and present as a thing made can be and recycled. So, synthesis doesn't merely suggest an ongoing process based in intermittent instances of unity.

Viz. apposite positions, you, said Martian, may wish to ask why this seemingly redundant process should occur at all. You may, in fact, employ a battlefield metaphor to invoke my neglect of efficacy or practicality in considering myself a maker. [Why do we assume that interstellar contexts will brook warfare at all? And we do.] Why? To participate categorically is the desire that has nothing to do with ambition. And, isn't A Tonalism emphatically post-ambition? Or, are there only a tonalists?

3. Our Commonality

A Tonalist was always a way of looking at writing in retrospect. In some cases the work was in the moment as work by myself or friends or people unknown to me whose work I admire or who happened to read the blog and get it. In other cases, it was by people who are dead, as my first husband Jerry Estrin, who died in 1993, or by others longer gone. As mentioned above, a moment of particularly intense motivation occurred when Norma Cole had a stroke almost a decade after Jerry's death. When that happened and it wasn't clear what the outcome would be, I became aware of wanting to have a way to speak about our writing and that of others whose work we valued. In a way, A Tonalist began simply as an expression of love. "Our Commonality," to use Jerry Estrin's title of a piece he wrote not long before his death, is our mortality and our willingness to witness each other's actions in relation to it. Perhaps our common task is to go as far into this witnessing as possible while retaining the ability to come back. Or maybe we don't come back. In a way, A Tonalist has always been a thinking about physicality and death, in relation to some of the work that I write and read and am surrounded by. An interrogation and framing of what we think in relation to each other.

That was in the spring of 2003. I wrote much of A Tonalist in the next few years, arguing for the poetics while and by enacting them. *Self-Destruction* came out in 2004. I was trying to complete my science fiction novel *Ultravioleta* which appeared in 2006. Ideally, I should include the publications history of several friends here. At times their books seem to prove the point and influence me more than mine do. During all this, I started another collection of short pieces called *Divination*, now almost complete. My relationships with younger writers increased in intensity and in number, both in teaching and in the poetry scene. Working as I do at a Bay Area poetry destination for locals and visitors alike, I seem to have many lunches with poets, not to mention long chats in the warehouse. I don't believe I have ever suggested that anyone be A Tonalist even when it was obvious that they were. Okay, maybe once. It rarely comes up. When it occasionally does come up I see it more as an opportunity to ask questions than to answer them.

The A Tonalist Notes blog, begun in 2005, was, as mentioned above, an experiment to find out if there actually was anything to this A Tonalist idea I had been writing into for a couple of years. A Tonalist Notes has always been a group blog though, with some exceptions, joining it has been more a symbolic action for most writers than an agreement to post comments. Some discussion occurred, as much in the world as in the blog, but I was never eager to characterize A Tonalist with any specificity and it wasn't a technique or a style so it remained a possibility. With some amusement but little surprise, I noticed a distinct aversion to being called A Tonalist among most of the writers whose work I regarded as A Tonalist. The older ones had perhaps been bruised by the poetry wars (in which people were included or discluded in groups to their distress, epithets were hurled, relationships strained, accusations made etc.) or they were independent or were already calling themselves something else. The younger people seemed to have a bit of all of the above and maybe they also wanted to keep all of their options open. Andrew Joron regards himself as a Surrealist but contributes to the A Tonalist blog. When I told Renee Gladman of A Tonalist at a teahouse in New York, she wondered if my work actually fit into the poetics I was describing (though she claims now not to remember this exchange). I very much enjoyed Renee's suspicion but think that my poetics do fit into the idea of A Tonalist. Lately I seem to be writing strangely linear fiction but lyric, or anti-lyric, is something that will remain part of my writing practice, even though I know better.

Some of the people mentioned above are part of the nonsite collective, where Kevin Killian's talk about the Spicer archives and the index cards took place. The collective is both a website and an event series taking place at multiple venues in San Francisco. I am not aware that they regard themselves as A Tonalist but I have written about various members of the nonsite collective (Taylor Brady, Rob Halpern and Jocelyn Saidenberg) in the A Tonalist blog and they have signed up as contributors. I regard these nuanced and yet passionate positions fondly and without insistence. My sense of A Tonalist was always tinged with a certain hilarity. If, at this or at any later point, you feel that you are being put on, fictionalized or in some way compromised, but continue to read anyway, you probably are an A Tonalist.

4. Our Rage, Our Cake

"Our Rage" is just another poem in *Divination*. In a way, the title is a trick or a puzzle but in another way it refers to the rage that exists in the texts and contexts we are in. Perhaps our age is the one in which negativity can be invoked as a way of encouraging access to the work. It is a new terrifying view of success. Does the emptiness of the houses below suggest that we are the audience Brent Cunningham invokes and that we dwell in the negative, shadowy, doubtful, open, vexed, private and yet public fullness intimated by A Tonalist? When I try to write about A Tonalist my efforts quickly devolve into poetry, often not even my own. So be it. Should I include more names here? Better not. End, instead, by replacing Spicer's trope of inedible silverware with Brent's cake from his book *Bird & Forest*.

But there comes the terrifying aspect, which we have avoided. As the man finishes, he turns to his private darkness, identifying his desire. He speaks it inwardly. Over and over he will be asked what was his wish, but can never divulge it. Thus he sees no authority touches him, no other soul, except by the whim of human need.

What really happens? What happens in the material itself?

The audience accepts the cake, eating it resentfully or cautiously. His year becomes them, and they are content.

How merry we are when the cake fills and becomes us. Never does anyone ask what it means to "become" a cake. What was the cake before, and what are we?

But it has made them satisfied, finally very comfortable. With his life dispersed among them, they go back to their empty houses.

Sources

Albon, George. *Empire Life*. Los Angeles: Littoral Books, 1998.

Aragon, Louis. *Nightwalker (La Paysan de Paris)* Translated by Frederick Brown. Englewood Cliffs, New Jersey: Prentice-Hall, 1970.

Auping, Michael. *Jess: A Grand Collage, 1951–1993*. Buffalo: Albright Knox Art Gallery, 1993.

Baghdad Burning. Anonymous blog.

Bell, Adrienne Baxter. *George Inness and the Visionary Landcape*. New York: George Braziller, 2007.

Berkson, Bill. "Philip Whalen," Rothenberg, Michael and Winson, Suzi, Eds. *Continuous Flame: A Tribute to Philip Whalen*. New York: Fish Drum, 2005.

Bertoff, Robert, Ed. *The Letters of Robert Duncan and Denise Levertov*. Stanford, CA: Stanford University Press, 2003.

Bird, Andrew. "Soval," *Mysterious Production of Eggs*. (album) Buffalo: Righteous Babe, 2005.

Blake, William. *The Complete Poetry & Prose of William Blake*. Garden City, NY: Doubleday & Company, 1970.

Bout, Danjel. *365 and a Wakeup*, blog.

Boonma, Montien. *Temple of the Mind*. New York: Asia Ink/Asia Society, 2003.

Brady, Taylor. *Microclimates*. San Francisco: Krupskaya, 2001.

---- *Yesterday's News*. New York: Factory School, 2005.

Brady, Taylor and Halpern, Rob. *Snow Sensitive Skin*. Oakland: Attics/Finch, 2007.

Brathwaite, Kamau. *Zea Mexican Diary*. Madison, WI: University of Wisconsin Press, 1993.

Buzzeo, Melissa. *What Began Us*. Providence, RI: Leon Works, 2007.

Cage, John. *A Week of Mondays*. Middletown, CT: Wesleyan, 1967.

---- *Silence*. Middletown, CT: Wesleyan, 1961.

Carr, Caleb. *Angel of Darkness*. New York: Ballantine Books, 1998.

Cole, Norma. *Where Shadows Will: Selected Poems 1988-2008*. San Francisco: City Lights Books, 2009.

---- *Natural Light*. New York: Libellum, 2009.

---- *a little a & a*. Los Angeles: Seeing Eye Books, 2002.

---- *Spinoza in Her Youth*. Richmond, CA: Omnidawn Publications, 2002.

---- *Mars*. Berkeley, CA: Listening Chamber, 1994.

---- *Contrafact*, Potes & Poets Press, 1996.

Cooper, Suzanne Fagence. *Pre-Raphaelite Art*. New York: Harry N. Abrams, Inc, 2003.

Courcil, Jacques. *Minimal Brass*. New York: Tzadik. (CD and conversations).

Cunningham, Brent. *Bird & Forest*. Brooklyn: Ugly Duckling Presse, 2005.

DJ Spooky. Interview on National Public Radio.

Dorsky, Nathaniel. *Devotional Cinema*. Berkeley, CA: Tuumba Press, 2005.

Dōgen. *Master Dogen's Shobogenzo*, Book 1. Woods Hole, MA: Windbell Publications, 1994.

Duncan, Michael and Kristine McKenna. *Semina Culture: Wallace Berman & His Circle*. Santa Monica, CA: Santa Monica Museum of Art, 2005.

Duncan, Robert and Spicer, Jack. *An Ode and Arcadia*. Berkeley, CA: Ark Press, 1974.

Durgin, Patrick. *Color Music*. Buffalo: Cuneiform Press, 2002.

---- "Imitation Poems," *Litmus Redact*, manuscript.

Estrin, Jerry. "Citizen's Dash," *Rome, A Mobile Home*. New York: Roof Books, 1993.

---- *In Motion Speaking*. San Francisco: Chance Additions, 1986.

Ferguson, Helaman with Ferguson, Claire. *Eightfold Way* (sculpture). Mathematical Science Research Institute Building, Shiing-Chen Chern Hall, University of California, Berkeley.

Gladman, Renee. *The Activist*. San Francisco: Krupskaya, 2003.

Gordon, Michael R. "An Army of One," *New York Times Magazine*. August 20, 2006.

Greenberg, Karen J. *The Torture Papers: The Road to Abu Ghraib*. Cambridge: Cambridge University Press, 2005.

Halsey, Alan. *Marginalien*. Hereford, Herefordshire, England: Five Seasons Press, 2005.

---- "On Poetic, 1980-82," A Tonalist blog, November 9, 2005.

---- *Memory Screen*, bound album, gift of the artist.

Harris, Bruce S. *The Collected Drawings of Beardsley*. New York: Bounty Books, 1967.

Hofer, Jen and Durgin, Patrick. *The Route*. Berkeley, CA: Atelos, 2008.

Hocquard, Emmanuel. "This Story Is Mine: Little Autobiographical Dictionary of Elegy," *Crosscut Universe: Writing on Writing from France*, edited by Norma Cole. Providence, RI: Burning Deck, 2000.

Jones, Harvey L. *Twilight and Reverie: California Tonalist Painting, 1890–1930*. Oakland: The Oakland Museum, 1995.

Joron, Andrew. *The Removes*. Lenox, MA: Hard Press, 1999.

---- *Fathom*. New York: Black Square Editions, 2003.

Lu, Pamela. *Ambient Parking Lot*. Chicago: Kenning Editions, forthcoming.

---- *The Second to Last Country*, New York: A Rest Press (chapbook), 2003.

Mac Low, Jackson. *Stanzas for Iris Lezak*. Barton, VT: Something Else Press, 1971.

Mehmedinovic, Semezdin. *Sarajevo Blues*. Translated by Ammiel Alcalay. San Francisco: City Lights, 2001.

Miller, Kathleen. *The Weather is Happening All Around Us*. Montreal: Delirium Press, 2006.

Moriarty, Laura et al. A Tonalist Notes, blog.

Moriarty, Laura. *Ultravioleta,* Berkeley, CA: Atelos, 2007

---- *Self-Destruction*. Sausalito, CA: Post-Apollo Press, 2006.

---- *Divination*. manuscript.

Morrison, Yedda. *Crop*. Berkeley, CA: Kelsey St. Press, 2002.

Morton, Oliver. *Mapping Mars*. New York: Picador, 2002.

Niedecker, Lorine. *Lorine Niedecker: Collected Works*. Berkeley, CA: University of California Press, 2002.

Pessoa, Fernando. *Always Astonished: Selected Prose*. San Francisco: City Lights, 1988.

Pound, Ezra. *Personae: Collected Shorter Poems*. New York: New Directions, 1971.

Saidenberg, Jocelyn. *Cusp*. Berkeley, CA: Kelsey St. Press, 2001.

Saunders, E. Dale. *Mudrā; A Study of Symbolic Gestures in Japanese Buddhist Sculpture*. New York: Pantheon Books, 1960.

Schaefer, Standard. *Bermuda Antigua*, manuscript.

Scharf, Mike. *For Kid Rock/Total Freedom*. New York: Spectacular Books, 2007.

Silliman, Ron. *Under Albany*. London: Salt Publishing, 2004.

---- Silliman's Blog.

Spicer, Jack. *My Vocabulary Did This to Me: The Collected Poetry of Jack Spicer*. Middletown, CT: Wesleyan University Press, 2008.

---- "Dialogue of Eastern and Western Poetry," Miriam Nichols, Ed.

Even On Sunday: Essays, Readings and Archival Materials on the Poetry and Poetics of Robin Blaser. Orono, ME: National Poetry Foundation, 2002.

---- *The Collected Books of Jack Spicer.* Los Angeles: Black Sparrow Press, 1975.

St. Thomasino, Gregory Vincent. *Logoclasody Manifesto, E.Ratio,* online journal, eratiopostmodernpoetry.com/pdfs

Steiner, Konrad. Email.

Thich Nhat Hahn. *Breathe! You Are Alive! Sutra on the Full Awareness of Breathing.* Berkeley: CA: Parallax Press, 1996.

Tremblay-McGaw, Robin. "Worldstruck, with an instrument: an interview with Norma Cole," XPoetics blog, March 4, 2009.

Vincent, Glyn. *The Unknown Night: The Genius and Madness of R.A. Blakelock, An American Painter.* New York: Grove Press, 2003.

Weiss, Peter. *Aesthetics of Resistance, vol. I.* Durham, NC: Duke University Press, 2005.

Whalen, Philip. *Kindness of Strangers.* Bolinas, CA: Four Seasons Foundation, 1976.

Tellerman, Esther. *Mental Ground*, translated by Keith Waldrop. Providence, RI: Burning Deck, 2002.

Wong Kar-Wai. *Ashes of Time*, film, 1994.

Warren, Alli. *Hounds*, self-published chapbook, Santa Cruz, CA, 2005.

Wolff, June. *Delta Primer: A Field Guide to the California Delta.* San Francisco: William Stout Publishers, 2003.

Laura Moriarty is the author of eleven books of poetry, including *A Semblance: Selected and New Poems, 1975–2007*, as well as the novels *Cunning* (1999) and *Ultravioleta* (2006). Recent chapbooks include *An Air Force* (2008) and *Ladybug Laws* (2009). Her awards include the Poetry Center Book Award in 1983, a Wallace Alexander Gerbode Foundation Award in Poetry in 1992, a 1998 New Langton Arts Award in Literature, and a Fund for Poetry grant in 2007. Moriarty is Deputy Director of Small Press Distribution in Berkeley, California, and has taught at Mills College and Naropa University, among other places. Currently, she is working with Standard Schaefer on a prose and poetry project with the working title, *The Feralist Papers or A Tonalist Manifesto*. For more, see the blog A Tonalist Notes.

NIGHTBOAT BOOKS, a nonprofit organization, seeks to develop audiences for writers whose work resists convention and transcends boundaries. We publish books rich with poignancy, intelligence, and risk. Please visit our website, www.nightboat.org, to learn more about us and how you can support our future publications.

The Lives of a Spirit/Glasstown: Where Something Got Broken
    by Fanny Howe

The Truant Lover by Juliet Patterson
    (Winner of the 2004 Nightboat Poetry Prize)

Radical Love: Five Novels by Fanny Howe

Glean by Joshua Kryah (Winner of the 2005 Nightboat Poetry Prize)

The Sorrow And The Fast Of It by Nathalie Stephens

Envelope of Night: Selected and Uncollected Poems, 1966-1990
    by Michael Burkard

In the Mode of Disappearance by Jonathan Weinert
    (Winner of the 2006 Nightboat Poetry Prize)

Your Body Figured by Douglas A. Martin

Dura by Myung Mi Kim

The All-Purpose Magical Tent by Lytton Smith
    (Winner of the 2007 Nightboat Poetry Prize)

Absence Where As (Claude Cahun and the Unopened Book)
    by Nathanaël (Nathalie Stephens)

Tiresias: The Collected Poems by Leland Hickman

In the Function of External Circumstances by Edwin Torres

)((eco (lang)(uage(reader)) edited by Brenda Iijima

Poetic Intention by Édouard Glissant

Ghost Fargo by Paula Cisewski

This book was made possible by a grant from the Topanga Fund, which is dedicated to promoting the arts and literature of California.

The following individuals have supported the publication of this book. We thank them for their generosity and commitment to the mission of Nightboat Books:

Sarah Heller
Elizabeth Motika
Benjamin Taylor

In addition, this book has been made possible, in part, by a grant from the New York State Council on the Arts Literature Program.

green press
INITIATIVE

Nightboat Books is committed to preserving ancient forests and natural resources. We elected to print this title on 30% postconsumer recycled paper, processed chlorine-free. As a result, for this printing, we have saved:

2 Trees (40' tall and 6-8" diameter)
1 Million BTUs of Total Energy
175 Pounds of Greenhouse Gases
841 Gallons of Wastewater
51 Pounds of Solid Waste

Nightboat Books made this paper choice because our printer, Thomson-Shore, Inc., is a member of Green Press Initiative, a nonprofit program dedicated to supporting authors, publishers, and suppliers in their efforts to reduce their use of fiber obtained from endangered forests.

For more information, visit www.greenpressinitiative.org

Environmental impact estimates were made using the Environmental Defense Paper Calculator. For more information visit: www.edf.org/papercalculator